W9-BNV-771

DRILL FOR SKILL

By C. C. RICKETT

Head of the English Department
Sarasota Public Schools
Sarasota, Florida

Formerly, Head of the English Department
South Kortright High School
South Kortright, New York

Dedicated to serving

AMSCO

our nation's youth

When ordering this book, please specify:

either N 346 P

or DRILL FOR SKILL

Amsco School Publications, Inc.
315 Hudson Street   New York, N. Y. 10013

ISBN 0-87720-327-X

Copyright 1946 Amsco School Publications, Inc.

Copyright renewed 1973 by Amsco School Publications, Inc.

———

*No part of this book may be reproduced
in any form without written permission
from the publisher.*

PRINTED IN THE UNITED STATES OF AMERICA

Foreword

There are two aspects to learning the use of any kind of tool, no matter what its type—a knowledge of its fundamental theory, and actual practice in its manipulation. This holds true in the field of English as well as in mechanics.

Only too often the classroom teacher concentrates on the study of the principles of English, and spends too little time in their practical application to everyday speech. Expecting good performance from this instruction is like teaching music theory to a student sitting beside a piano, and failing to provide time to use the keyboard.

Regardless of his theoretical knowledge, a piano student gets nowhere without continued practice. The English student who knows only the governing principle has not completed his job either. He needs to practice until the correct application of that principle becomes as automatic as the multiplication table. He needs to be able to say "he doesn't" instead of "he don't," instinctively, *without* thinking.

The author of this book is a classroom teacher who knows the boys and girls for whom he writes. There is no abstract theory in his completed work. We saw these drills used and revised, re-used and revamped again, day after day in his own classes, while he was head of the English Department in this school. Only the material that actually produced results was retained, and that after it had been checked again and again to make sure that it did develop the answers to real problems in students' daily speech.

The author realizes well that there are certain fundamental principles which need to be reasoned out. These are to be taught until they are *understood,* never drilled. Their applications must be recognized and used again and again, repeatedly, until there is correct habit. The drills presented are clear, simple, thorough, and progressive. They have worked in the author's own classes. We are confident that they will work in other teachers' classes as well.

M. W. MULDOON, *Principal*
Waverly Junior High School
Waverly, New York

Contents

1. Nouns

According to the kind of work words do in a sentence, all words are divided into eight classes called *parts of speech.* The eight parts of speech are the following: nouns, pronouns, adjectives, verbs, adverbs, prepositions, conjunctions and interjections. To tell the part of speech of any word in a sentence, you must first determine what kind of work the word does or what idea it expresses.

A **noun** is the name of a person, place, thing or quality. Nouns are classified as proper, common, collective, abstract.

A **proper noun** is the individual name of a particular person, place or thing. A proper noun should always begin with a capital letter.

> Mary, Miami, Rover, Pacific Ocean, the Bible, Tuesday, Mr. Bond

A **common noun** is the general name of any one of a class of persons, places or things.

> girl, city, dog, school, plane, editor-in-chief

A **collective noun** is the name of the whole group or collection of persons or things.

> crew, herd, team, family, army, union

An **abstract noun** is the name of a quality of an object or of a general characteristic of a person or thing.

> redness, hardness, honesty, beauty, cheerfulness

Exercise 1: Nouns—Part I

Select the *nouns* in the following sentences:

1. The sun rose over Lake Wales.
2. The jury has decided the fate of John Gray.
3. The family spent the holiday at the beach.
4. Florida is bordered by the Atlantic Ocean and the Gulf of Mexico.
5. A pack of hungry wolves invaded the camp.
6. The band will play at the game Saturday.
7. The boys caught three black bass.
8. The whiteness of the sand blinded us.

9. Next Thursday will be Thanksgiving Day.

10. Mrs. James showed them the way to the lake.
11. Patience is a virtue.
12. America is truly the home of the brave.
13. The mob was outside the house.
14. Freedom and justice are our guiding principles.
15. The pilot of the plane is from Detroit.
16. The University of Michigan is a very old institution.
17. Key West is the city of Florida nearest to South America.
18. A crowd of men gathered around Mr. Johnson as he demonstrated his new invention.
19. The next meeting will be held in January.
20. Spring is the season of the year I like best.

Exercise 2: Nouns—Part II

Select the *nouns* in the following sentences:

1. A horde of bandits attacked the camp.
2. Sarasota is the winter quarters of Ringling Brothers Circus.

3. Into the bay sailed the victorious fleet.

4. The family is at Long Beach for a vacation.
5. The darkness of the sky warned us of a storm.
6. In Deland we find the John B. Stetson University.
7. Buffalo is a large city in New York.
8. A swarm of bees flew past us.
9. The Statue of Liberty is in New York Harbor.
10. My sister will start school this fall.
11. We saw a squadron of planes.
12. Health is one of our most precious gifts.
13. Beauty is not one of the essential points in judging a person.
14. Mr. Lopez took the children to the ballgame.
15. The fierceness of the attack took the enemy by surprise.
16. In August I expect to visit Uncle Harry who lives in Chicago.
17. Shakespeare was one of the greatest dramatists of all times.
18. St. Augustine is the oldest city in North America.
19. Last Sunday, Joe and I visited a sick friend at the hospital.
20. A large pack of coyotes did much damage.

2. Pronouns

A **pronoun** is a word used in place of a noun. Pronouns are classified as personal, interrogative, demonstrative, indefinite, relative, possessive, reflexive and reciprocal.

A **personal pronoun** refers to the speaker (first person), or to the person spoken to (second person), or to the person or thing spoken about (third person).

First Person: I, me, we, us

Second Person: you

Third Person: he, him, she, her, they, them, it

An **interrogative pronoun** is used in asking a question: who? whom? which? what? whose?

Who called me?   *Which* do you like?

What is it?   *Whose* are you using?

A **demonstrative pronoun** points out a particular person, place or thing previously mentioned.

Singular	*Plural*
this, that	these, those
This is mine.	You may have *these*.

An **indefinite pronoun** does not clearly point out any particular person, place or thing. Some indefinite pronouns are: each, some, any, either, neither, one, all, both, someone, anyone, no one, none, everyone, anybody, nobody, somebody, few, others, many.

Some were lost.   *Few* are present.

A **relative pronoun** connects the dependent (or subordinate) clause with the independent (or principal) clause. The common relative pronouns are:

who, whose and *whom* refer to persons
which and *what* refer to animals and things
that refers to persons, animals and things
He is the boy *who* (or *that* but not *which* or *what*)
    helped me.
Is this the pen *which* (or *that*) you lost?

Every relative pronoun is used in two ways: (1) it is used in its own clause as subject or as direct object; (2) it also joins the clause in which it stands with its antecedent.

A **possessive pronoun** denotes ownership or possession. Some common possessive pronouns are: mine, his, hers, its, ours, yours, theirs. (*Caution:* Never use an apostrophe with possessive pronouns because they are already possessive in form.)

This book is *mine*.   *Hers* is lost.

Note: My, their, our, your and her are possessive adjectives and not possessive pronouns, because they are always used to modify a noun or pronoun. For example: *my* coat, *their* hats, *our* team, etc.

A **reflexive pronoun** is used as an object, and denotes the same person or thing as the subject. The reflexive pronouns are: myself, yourself, himself, herself, itself, themselves, ourselves, yourselves.

I hurt *myself*.   She spoke to *herself*.

Reciprocal pronouns are the phrases *each other* and *one another*. They are reciprocal because they signify interchange, or reciprocity, of actions or feelings. *Each other* refers to two persons; *one another* refers to more than two.

The two girls read to *each other*.

All the people in the neighborhood seemed to enjoy helping *one another*.

Exercise 3: Pronouns—Part I

Select the *pronouns* in the following sentences:

1. Are you the boy who left early?
2. They enjoyed themselves at the movies last night.
3. What was the cause of the accident?
4. Did you see him or her at the concert?
5. They always help one another.
6. This is the girl who will sing for us.
7. Few came but many were invited.

8. The dog that barked gave us a warning.

9. Don't you think he contradicted himself?
10. Which do you want?
11. These are the plants which I bought yesterday.
12. I expect someone to call me.
13. Who spoke to you?
14. Marion and I gave gifts to each other on Christmas.
15. These are the ones.
16. Which do you like?
17. Either will be satisfactory, don't you think?
18. Are these yours?
19. They hurt themselves on the slide.
20. These are hers, not his.

Exercise 4: Pronouns—Part II

Select the *pronouns* in the following sentences:

1. She hurt herself.
2. Someone left it here.
3. She takes her work seriously.
4. Who is the girl who was with you yesterday?
5. Someone left a package for you.

6. He is a boy whom everyone likes.

7. I believe the two girls wrote to each other regularly.
8. Which of these do you want?
9. This is the store that I told you about.
10. Yours is newer than mine, I noticed.
11. I enjoyed the program, but others didn't seem to care for it.
12. The ball of wool unwound itself as I dropped it
13. Both were at fault, but neither would admit it.
14. Whose are these?
15. What did he do?
16. The book which I read yesterday is his.
17. They gave it to us.
18. Others have done this before you.
19. What did they tell you?
20. Is that his or mine?

3. Adjectives

An **adjective** is a word used to modify a noun or pronoun. An adjective describes or limits the noun or pronoun it modifies.

A. Descriptive adjectives tell the quality, kind or condition of a person, place or thing. Proper adjectives begin with capital letters because they are derived from the particular name of a person, place or country.

a *large* boat   on the *busy* street
the *American* flag   the *Irish* tenor

Note: Some participles may be used as ordinary adjectives.

a *used* car   a *running* motor

B. Limiting adjectives fall into the following classes: demonstrative, indefinite, relative, possessive and interrogative.

Demonstrative adjectives are: this, that, these, those, the. (*The* is sometimes called the definite article. It is usually less emphatic than the other demonstrative adjectives.)

This book is mine.   *These* flowers are pretty.

Indefinite adjectives are: any, all, another, every, each, either, neither, few, many, numerous, other, no, some, several, such, various, a, an. (*A* and *an* are called the indefinite articles.)

I have *many* friends.

Several girls were late to school.

Relative adjectives are: which, whichever, what, whatever.

I explained his algebra, for *which* help he was very grateful.

He always does *whatever* work he promises.

Possessive adjectives are: his, her, its, my, our, your, their, whose, one's, one another's, each other's.

This is *his* book.

My brother is in the Navy.

Interrogative adjectives are: which? what? whose?

Which color do you like?

Whose book is this?

Numerical adjectives denote quantity or order.

Quantity: one, two, three, etc.

Order: first, second, third, etc.

Exercise 5: Adjectives—Part I

Select the *adjectives* in the following sentences:

1. My mother said I may have whichever dress I desire.
2. This red book is yours.
3. Long lines of tired people stood in front of the ticket office.
4. The little acorn grows into the mighty oak.
5. Into the angry water plunged the frightened horses.
6. Do you like ripe olives?

7. Is this your Spanish book?

8. Which dish do you want?
9. Two men are waiting in your office.
10. The speeding motorist was stopped by a motorcycle policeman.
11. The dog hurt its paw.
12. This is an interesting story.
13. Those apples are for sale.
14. His dog is a small black Scottie.
15. Isn't this a beautiful day?

16. The ripe fruit hung from the trees.
17. With my compass, I drew a perfect circle.
18. The three small boys made more noise than the twenty girls.
19. Gay colored streamers flew from every window.
20. Huge red flames shot out from the burning building.

Exercise 6: Adjectives—Part II

Select the *adjectives* in the following sentences:

1. The dripping water annoyed my mother.

2. The high cold waves dashed upon the rocky shore.
3. Whose flowers are in this blue vase?
4. On the third day of our trip, we drove two hundred miles.
5. Huge vicious waves dashed against our frail boat.
6. We liked the highly-polished finish of the rare old chair.

7. A mysterious sound issued from the unlighted house.
8. Her room was always in perfect order.
9. She lost my new blue sweater, for which loss she cried.
10. Do not leave your coats on the hot radiator.
11. On the steep grassy hillside, grazed the contented herd.
12. Which flavor did you say you prefer?
13. A shining new car stood in front of our house.
14. Does your pen have a fine point?
15. You may have whichever pencil is in the top drawer.
16. A clear loud call rang out in the still night.
17. Our new car does not fit into our small garage.
18. At last we came to a winding, narrow, jagged gorge.
19. The two boys caught twenty large black bass.

20. In the polar regions, the people live in igloos.

4. Verbs

A **verb** is a word that—

1. shows *action* and tells what the subject does.

    I *hit* the mark.   He *walked* to school.

2. shows the *position* or *state of being* of the subject.

    I *am* in the   She *felt* better.
    kitchen.

Auxiliary verbs are helping verbs. They are: can, be, do, have, shall, will, may, must, etc. They are used as helpers to form the tense of the main verb.

    You *may stand* up.   They *have left* the room.

Exercise 7: Verbs—Part I

Select the *verbs* in the following sentences:

1. I tasted the food.
2. He has since become a famous artist.
3. We will stroll through the park.
4. He dashed out and bought some sandwiches.
5. Father bought us a new car.
6. They all shouted joyously.

7. I have been helping him.
8. Shall I assist you?
9. These waves are high.
10. They were strangers.
11. Did the rope break while you were carrying the package?
12. Is this milk sour?
13. Don't wait for me.
14. Later we heard a crashing sound.
15. Do come over this afternoon.
16. Will you be riding in the coach?
17. You were elected by the class.
18. Where was it found?
19. John remained home, but Harry went to the game.
20. Keep them here.

Exercise 8: Verbs—Part II

Select the *verbs* in the following sentences:

1. We jumped into the waiting car and dashed off to the carnival.
2. The pitcher tossed three strikes in a row.
3. The crowd cheered excitedly.
4. Our team won the game.
5. Did they consult Mr. Bush before they undertook the work?
6. The plane glided smoothly to the airfield.

7. Some day we will take a trip out West.

8. The two men sat and talked for several hours before they realized that it was past dinner time.
9. The ground crew checked the engine.
10. Don't you ever get tired of swimming?
11. Put your books here.
12. I tossed and turned all night.
13. You would not enjoy the trip under those conditions.
14. Mary, you should have studied this lesson before you went home.
15. Have you ever seen a lemon tree?
16. Yes, we once had several in our back yard.
17. The ship has been newly decorated.
18. The sky was very black and we all feared a storm.
19. That work is easy, I think.
20. Could you not have come for this when you were notified?

5. Adverbs

An **adverb** is a word that modifies a verb, an adjective or another adverb.

> They ran *quickly.*
> (*quickly* modifies the verb *ran*)

> She is a *strikingly* beautiful girl.
> (*strikingly* modifies the adjective *beautiful*)

> Mary sang *very* well.
> (*very* modifies the adverb *well*)

Adverbs answer the questions: when? where? why? how? how many times? to what extent?

Some common adverbs are: soon, often, also, too, not, then, now, yet, here, again, once, there, slowly, thus, still, almost, somewhat, hardly, finally.

> The sun shone *brightly.*   I *often* write to John.

Exercise 9: Adverbs—Part I

Select the *adverbs* in the following sentences:

1. He left the room immediately.

2. It was a very difficult test.
3. Finally the teacher read the play aloud.
4. Billy reads slowly but very clearly and pleasingly.
5. You are walking too rapidly.
6. Haltingly, the old man told his story.
7. I think it is uncomfortably warm today.
8. I was sorry I had not returned sooner.
9. The child gazed longingly at the very tempting sundae.
10. I did not leave; I had not entirely finished the work.
11. There they go now.
12. Finally I found the combination.
13. I have been often asked that question.
14. Up went the curtain and down went our spirits.
15. He spoke somewhat hesitatingly.

16. The phone rang again; this time I quickly answered it.

17. Will they build there again?
18. We chose a rather cool day for swimming.
19. Don't do it now.
20. Don't speak so rapidly.

Exercise 10: Adverbs—Part II

Select the *adverbs* in the following sentences:

1. Don't talk so loudly, boys.
2. I often stop here for a light lunch.
3. He has done very well; don't you agree?
4. Always walk slowly in the halls.
5. Dad sometimes plays tennis with us.
6. I often forget my new phone number.
7. The girl walked up and down.
8. You spoke too hastily.
9. This is an uncommonly cool day for June.
10. Finally I finished my homework and immediately went to Dick's house.
11. I can't remember the day I went there.
12. She rocked slowly and sang very softly to herself.
13. She surely sings very sweetly.
14. They have written it twice now.
15. Do you often read during the evening?
16. Helen is an unusually tall girl.
17. She speaks too quickly.
18. I hardly recognized him.
19. Louise washed the dishes unwillingly.
20. Wasn't this a very easy lesson?

6. *Prepositions*

A **preposition** is a word or phrase that shows the relation between the noun that it takes as an object and some other word in the sentence.

Some common prepositions are:

aboard	between	on
about	beyond	on account of
above	but (meaning	out
according to	except)	out of
across	by	outside
after	by means of	regarding
along	by way of	since
amid	down	throughout
amidst	during	to
among	except	toward
around	for	under
as for	from	until
at	in	up
because of	inside	upon
before	into	with
behind	of	within
beneath	off	without

The preposition together with its object and the modifiers of the object is called a **prepositional phrase.**

> The boy fell *off the boat.*
>> (*off the boat* is the prepositional phrase and is used to modify *fell; off* is the preposition; *boat* is the object of the preposition; *the* modifies *boat*)

> Helen went *to the corner store.*
>> (*to the corner store* is the prepositional phrase and is used to modify *went; to* is the preposition; *store* is the object of the preposition; *the* and *corner* modify *store*)

Exercise 11: Prepositions—Part I

In each of the following sentences, *(a)* select the *prepositional phrase* and *(b)* underline once the *preposition* and twice the *object of the preposition:*

1. They put the package on the table.
2. Around the corner came the car.
3. Aboard the ship were many college students.
4. The man jumped quickly out the window and ran hastily down the street and into an alley.
5. Inside the house could be heard shouts of laughter.
6. They camped among the palms.
7. Everything went according to plan.
8. John fell off the dock.
9. During the winter we went to Miami Beach.

10. All came to the party but Jack and his sister.
11. From my chair on the porch, I could see down the street to the bank.
12. We walked slowly along the beach and into the clubhouse.
13. Behind us lay the valley covered with deep snow.
14. From beneath the pier a cry was heard.
15. As for me, I don't care for it.
16. The game was canceled on account of rain.
17. Amid the shouting of the crowd, Jerry's cries were not heard.
18. Did you call regarding the apartment?
19. Beneath the window was a garden of flowers.
20. All remained except Mr. and Mrs. Shaw.

Exercise 12: Prepositions—Part II

In each of the following sentences, (a) select the *prepositional phrase* and (b) underline once the *preposition* and twice the *object of the preposition:*

1. They all went aboard the train.
2. By means of code, the spies relayed their messages to headquarters.
3. The boys camped out during the months of July and August.
4. He told us about the plans for our vacation.
5. Within an hour the flames were beyond control.
6. Is this the first day of spring?

7. It is very true that we learn from experience.
8. The flyer landed the plane in the center of the field without any mishap.
9. A stream of water trickled down the side of the mountain.
10. He has succeeded by means of hard work.
11. Amidst the confusion, I heard the sound of a siren.
12. They will remain until June or July.
13. They will go by way of Atlanta.
14. Throughout the night the wind howled about the house.
15. Outside the city, signs of gardening were everywhere evident.
16. They have been there since dawn.
17. Beyond the plains, lay the snow-covered hills.
18. Because of the heat, we went home at two o'clock.
19. The dog slept beneath the cot.

20. He left without notice.

7. Conjunctions

A **conjunction** is a word that connects words, phrases or clauses. There are two classes of conjunctions:

Coordinate conjunctions connect words, phrases or clauses of the same rank or kind. The principal coordinate conjunctions are: and, or, nor, but.

Jane *and* Fred came last night.

Charles likes bread *but* James does not.

There are a few coordinate conjunctions (called **correlative conjunctions**) which are used in pairs: either . . . or, neither . . . nor, both . . . and, not only . . . but also, whether . . . or.

Both Fred *and* George are good musicians.

You must *either* come with us now *or* walk all the way.

Subordinate conjunctions connect a dependent (or subordinate) clause with the independent (or main) clause. Some subordinate conjunctions are: as, since, than, although, because, unless, before, that, when, while, for, where, though, as if, as soon as, after, however, therefore, in order that, if, whether.

Since he left, all has been very quiet.

Though I tried very hard, I could not lift the trunk.

Exercise 13: Conjunctions—Part I

Select the *conjunctions* in the following sentences:

1. Fruits and vegetables are plentiful now.
2. When it rains, we listen to the radio on the porch.
3. Either the dog or the cat scratched the chair.
4. Jack was my best friend and roommate for two years.
5. We shall go to the beach this summer or we shall rent a cottage on the lake.
6. The boys are reading or studying in their room.
7. After you left, we read for an hour.
8. Before you arrived, we heard a good program.
9. Unless you do more work, you will surely fail.
10. The dog growled fiercely whenever he heard a stranger approaching.
11. I did not go because I was not invited.
12. Since you are here early, you may help sort and distribute these papers.

13. My watch was slow; therefore, I was late this morning.
14. I have not seen the movie nor do I intend to.
15. Mother will stay here while you are away.
16. He lived and worked and died there.
17. I will be there before you, for you are always late
18. On Sunday we visited not only Bill but also Joe.
19. The children responded quickly and cheerfully.
20. Longfellow and Whittier are famous poets.

Exercise 14: Conjunctions—Part II

Select the *conjunctions* in the following sentences:

1. The game will go on whether you play or not.
2. Though he doesn't seem to spend much money, he is always in debt.
3. She invited not only Helen but also Frances.
4. If you go to Havana this summer, send me a card.
5. I earned more money than Fred or Gerald.
6. Neither money nor position seemed to interest him.
7. You may leave as soon as you have finished.
8. This store sells jewelry and books.
9. Whenever I think of that accident, I shudder.
10. Both Mr. Jones and his sister are teachers in our school.
11. If you do not know the road. you had better drive slowly.

12. Ralph sings better than his sister does.

13. She always remembers where she put her books at night.
14. Neither my father nor my mother drives a car.
15. After the sun went down, we took a long walk.
16. Our guests will come today or tomorrow, but they will leave on Saturday.
17. Papers, boxes and old books lay all about.
18. Unless something prevents it, we will leave Monday.
19. Try to make your themes both interesting and brief.
20. Yale and Harvard are old universities.

8. Interjections

An **interjection** is a word that shows strong or sudden feeling. Interjections have no grammatical relation to the sentence. Usually an interjection is followed by an exclamation mark, although sometimes it is followed by a comma. Some interjections are: ah, ha, oh, whew, bang, hist, listen, boo, hello, ouch, pshaw, alas, hurrah.

Ah! Now I see it!   *Oh,* let it go for now.

Exercise 15: Interjections

Select the *interjections* in the following sentences:

1. Oh! I dropped it.
2. Pshaw, I can't do it!
3. Whew! That took my breath away.
4. Ouch! That hurt!
5. She cried, "Ha! Ha! I caught you."
6. They all cried, "Boo! Boo!"
7. Listen! There it is again!
8. The audience all shouted, "Bravo!"
9. "Hist! Lie down!" said the scout as we drew near.
10. Ah! I know.

Exercise 16: Words Used As Different Parts of Speech—Part 1

Tell the *part of speech* of each italicized word according to the way it is used in the sentence:

1. Is this the *right* answer?
2. Turn to the *right* at the next corner.
3. He tried to *right* the overturned canoe.

4. The *inside* of the house was smoky.
5. It was in his *inside* pocket.
6. Let's step *inside* the house.
7. Did you go *inside*?

8. The children coasted *down* the hill.
9. He sat *down*.
10. It was a steep *down* grade.

11. Please *open* the door.
12. At last we came to *open* country.
13. It is always pleasant to have an outing in the *open*

14. The *sound* frightened us.
15. *Sound* the bell loudly.
16. You should have a *sound* body.

17. His *hand* was badly injured.
18. *Hand* me the book.

19. It will *cost* too much.
20. What was the original *cost*?

Exercise 17: Words Used As Different Parts of Speech—Part II

Tell the *part of speech* of each italicized word according to the way it is used in the sentence:

1. This is an *iron* box.
2. *Iron* is very valuable.
3. Did you *iron* this?

4. He dropped the *pin*.
5. *Pin* it up securely.
6. The *pin* tray is very valuable.

7. *Work* never hurt anyone.
8. The *work* sheet was spoiled.
9. Do you *work* every Saturday?

10. *Run* to the post-office.
11. The *run* was long and difficult.
12. The Music Hall is a first-*run* theater.

13. Mr. Briggs is a *near* relative.
14. The arrows fell *near*.
15. We found it *near* the brook.
16. They came from far and *near*.
17. As we *near* the camp, don't make a sound.

18. May I have the next *dance?*
19. I'd be glad to *dance* with you.
20. They make a fine *dance* team.

Exercise 18: Words Used As Different Parts of Speech—Part III

Tell the *part of speech* of each italicized word according to the way it is used in the sentence:

1. The enemy will probably *sack* the city.
2. We bought a *sack* of potatoes.

3. The *campaign* was successful.
4. The candidates will *campaign* for two weeks.
5. The *campaign* speech was inspiring.

6. The hunter *shot* the deer.
7. The *shot* landed in the right spot.

8. The *book* was nowhere to be found.
9. Did you *book* passage?
10. I gave him *book* ends on his birthday.

11. Do not *coast* when driving.
12. The *coast* guard was very busy.

13. He has a ten-day *leave.*
14. *Leave* them here.

15. *Club* that snake.
16. We will go to the *club* after school.
17. The *club* house is very noisy.

18. Time the race with a stop *watch.*
19. *Watch* it closely.
20. The *watch* tower was destroyed.

Exercise 19: Words Used As Different Parts of Speech—Part IV

Tell the *part of speech* of each italicized word according to the way it is used in the sentence:

1. The *empty* bottle lay on the floor.
2. *Empty* the box into the basket.
3. The dog tried to *mother* the kitten.
4. His *mother* came yesterday.
5. There was a *break* in the tire.
6. He will probably *break* the record.
7. Our *radio* station is WSUN.
8. *Radio* the message at once.
9. We bought a new *radio*.
10. How long did you *travel?*
11. *Travel* broadens your outlook on life.
12. Why don't you consult a *travel* bureau?
13. The *ice* is in the box.
14. We attended the *ice* carnival.
15. I will *ice* the tea.
16. I left my books *behind*.
17. The dog is sitting *behind* you.
18. Her father is a *letter* carrier.
19. You should *letter* the sign carefully.
20. Here is a *letter* to mail.

Exercise 20: Part of Speech of Each Word—Part I

Write the *part of speech* of each word in the following sentences:

1. The old house was sold.
2. They bought a used car.
3. What subjects are you taking?
4. My shoes are too tight.
5. The girls and boys sing very well.
6. Where did they go?
7. Put the letter where you will find it again.
8. He has been away from home since December.
9. The man drove rapidly up the street.
10. Harry was sorry about the scratch on his father's car.
11. Real jade is very valuable.
12. For an airplane, a lighter wood is needed.
13. A regiment of soldiers marched down the street.
14. While he was away, the postman called.
15. These boys are my friends.
16. Bill passed all his tests, but Mary failed in science.
17. The timid little boy and his very faithful dog walked slowly into the old house.
18. Throughout the long night, Frank kept careful watch over the little dog.
19. Both George and his teacher were there.
20. That is the house my father built.

Exercise 21: Part of Speech of Each Word—Part II

Write the *part of speech* of each word in the following sentences:

1. He played until he was tired.
2. The lesson was very clear and easy.
3. He sold it to me for one dollar.
4. Do you think this work is too easy?
5. The richness and softness of her voice thrilled the listeners.
6. Gay red streamers flew from every window.
7. I am very happy for I have had very good news.
8. This is a very hot day!
9. The tired child became very sleepy.
10. The sky seems very blue tonight.
11. Either you or I will go to the store for Mother.
12. I often stop here for a light lunch.
13. He left in December, and I have not seen him since.
14. His decision surprised even his best friends.
15. There stood the girl, happy and proud.
16. While we were packing, the phone rang.
17. He will not be here because he has an engagement.
18. Will you have your name engraved on it?
19. The icy roads made safe driving almost impossible.
20. Because I was tired, I did not enjoy the movie.

9. *Infinitives*

Verbals are words derived from verbs but which are used as other parts of speech. There are three kinds of verbals: infinitives, gerunds and participles.

An **infinitive** is a verbal noun used with *to:* to see, to hear, to hope.

An **infinitive phrase** is the infinitive with its modifier and object: to see you soon, to hear a radio program, to hope it clears up.

To may be omitted after let, need, bid, see, feel, please, hear, make, and a few other verbs.

> I heard him *(to) talk.*
> He made them *(to) sit* down.

Uses of the infinitive: An infinitive may be used as a noun, adjective or adverb.

As a noun:

> Subject—
> > *To skate* is fun.
> Object of the preposition—
> > John was about *to throw* the ball.

36

Direct object—

    She likes *to sing.*

Predicate nominative—

    Her plan was *to meet* us.

As an adjective:

    Here is a book *to read.*

As an adverb:

    He worked *to earn* his way through college.

Exercise 22: Infinitives—Part I

In each of the following sentences, *(a)* select the infinitive and *(b)* state its use in the sentence as a noun, adjective or adverb:

1. He tried to win.
2. They hoped to cross the river.
3. They went downstairs to discover the cause of the noise.
4. I wish to congratulate you.
5. Our greatest difficulty was to find a suitable house.
6. I ran to catch the train.
7. Our desire is to find him.
8. I want to finish it.
9. To carry the load seemed impossible.
10. Couldn't you spare some time to listen to me?
11. To bowl well requires much practice.

12. I want to spend a week there.
13. We all want to attend the play in January.
14. Here are some tomatoes to pick.
15. I can see no way except to call now.
16. It took Fred an hour to start his car.
17. Mary has tried to learn the game for several months.
18. Jerry worked hard to earn some spending money.
19. Please let her go to the movies with me.

20. Paul Revere rode to warn the settlers of the approach of the British.

Exercise 23: Infinitives—Part II

In each of the following sentences, *(a)* select the infinitive and *(b)* state its use in the sentence as a noun, adjective or adverb:

1. Would you like to meet Mary?
2. She hopes to become a resident of this city.
3. To see is not always to believe.
4. He stopped to tie his shoe.

5. A policeman's duty is to enforce the law.
6. His greatest desire is to be an aviator.
7. To see a good circus is to get a thrill.
8. There is a high mountain to scale.

9. You may not go.

10. She will have to buy something to wear to the wedding.
11. I went to the library to answer the phone.
12. My brothers hope to become lawyers.
13. To land this fish took great skill and patience.
14. Use this broom to sweep the floor.
15. Some of the pupils hoped to leave early.
16. It was her greatest desire to be an opera singer.
17. To build our camp took all summer.
18. The boys came running to see the parade.
19. I like to hear him sing.
20. I wanted to attend, but I was too busy.

10. Gerunds

A **gerund** is a verbal noun ending in *ing* which may be used as a noun. Since it is a verbal noun, it may also take an object. Examples of gerunds are:

> working, thinking, playing, reading, turning, marching

Examples of gerunds with an object are:

> playing a game, reading a book, taking a walk

Uses of the gerund:

Subject—
> *Spelling* is my easy subject.

Object of the preposition—
> She is proficient in *spelling*.

Direct object—
> I like *swimming*.

Predicate nominative—
> His hobby is *singing*.

Object of the infinitive—
> Mary expects to learn *typing*.

Exercise 24: Gerunds—Part I

In the following sentences, (a) select the gerund and (b) state its use in the sentence as subject, object of the preposition, etc.:

1. Do you like skating?
2. Climbing that mountain will not be very difficult.
3. The little boy began asking questions.
4. Decorating the room gave us great pleasure.
5. Bob likes fishing and rowing.
6. My parents are not opposed to dancing.
7. Wrapping packages soon became very tiresome.
8. He is not ashamed of his dislike for dancing.
9. Her favorite sport is bowling.
10. I am sure he is guilty of neglecting his school work,
11. Burt insisted on buying me the book.
12. Skiing is a favorite winter sport in the North.
13. I hope to learn typing.
14. He earned his way through college by working at the fraternity house.
15. Rowing a boat develops muscles.
16. His favorite sport is boxing.
17. My mother has always disliked washing dishes.
18. She teaches spelling and writing at one of our grade schools.
19. Are you fond of reading plays?
20. Speaking clearly is a business asset.

Exercise 25: Gerunds—Part II

In the following sentences, (a) select the gerund and (b) state its use in the sentence as subject, object of the preposition, etc.:

1. Hunting and fishing were his chief diversions.
2. I don't like picking berries.
3. At last they were successful in reaching the harbor.
4. He freed himself by twisting and turning.
5. Brisk walking is good exercise.
6. My greatest trouble was keeping my dog from barking.
7. We spent most of our time in looking for a room.
8. I expect to study printing.
9. Reading, writing and spelling kept his average low.
10. We bought heavy shoes for hiking over the trails.
11. My sister dislikes rowing a boat.
12. My favorite pastimes are swimming and dancing.
13. In the evening I enjoy reading a good novel.
14. Earning money last summer was not difficult.
15. We could hear the droning of the planes.
16. Caring for the poor was her greatest concern.
17. Mr. Banks taught boxing, wrestling and fencing.
18. My uncle Fred's vocation was planting different kinds of flowers.
19. To master spelling you must study hard.
20. Swimming is very good exercise.

11. Participles

A **participle** is a verbal adjective used to modify a noun or pronoun.

A **participial phrase** is a group of words introduced by a participle. A participial phrase consists of a participle, the object of the participle, if it has one, and any word modifying the participle.

The dog *eating the bone* is mine.
>(*eating the bone* is a participial phrase; *eating* is the participle; *eating the bone* modifies *dog*)

A participial phrase which precedes the subject should be followed by a comma.

Lying in the sun, I got very sleepy.
>(*Lying in the sun* modifies *I*)

The present participle ends in *ing,* the past participle in *d, ed, en* or *t.*

The tall man *carrying* the briefcase is Mr. Bim.
>(*carrying* is a present participle modifying *man*)

The lecture *given* by Dr. Hall interested us.
>(*given* is a past participle modifying *lecture*)

Exercise 26: Participles—Part I

In the following sentences, (*a*) select the participle and (*b*) state the word it modifies:

1. The wounded bird hopped along the sidewalk.
2. Lying in the sun that day, John forgot all his troubles.
3. This robe, made of silk, is quite expensive.
4. Carrying a heavy bag of potatoes, the child walked slowly.
5. The books, piled neatly on the desk, did not look untidy.
6. The boy riding the bicycle is my youngest brother.
7. Getting home so late, Father was tired.
8. The crowd pushed into the street, shouting and waving banners.
9. I love our back yard, filled with trees and flowers.
10. Feeling hungry, we ordered lunch brought to our room.
11. Seizing the ball, George made a basket.
12. Our teacher, aided by several pupils, raised a large sum for the Red Cross.
13. I could see the children running down the street.
14. The poems learned in early life are frequently long remembered.
15. We could see the old man coming slowly up the path.

16. In the cabin was a very cheery fire, crackling and glowing.
17. The moon, peeking from behind the high mountain, shone brilliantly.
18. Driving at break-neck speed, we soon arrived at the airport.
19. The old watch, lost four years ago, was hardly tarnished.
20. Wild dogs looking for food came into our camp last night.

Exercise 27: Participles—Part II

In the following sentences, (a) select the participle and (b) state the word it modifies:

1. The chickens, frightened by the noise, ran for shelter.
2. Being a large school, the Central Senior High is one of the leaders in athletics in this country.
3. My motor, choking and wheezing, did not sound very encouraging.

4. The old sailor sat on the wharf, gazing out to sea.

5. Being a star player, Ernest took part in the whole game.
6. The river, rising steadily, made us all very uneasy.
7. I sometimes like to hear the raindrops pattering on the roof.
8. My tomatoes, planted last month, will soon be ready to eat.
9. Lifting his hat, the boy politely entered the room.
10. The man standing on the corner is my English teacher.
11. Our cottage, built on the sand, has begun to settle.
12. Towering pines were all about us.
13. The little girls, dressed in white gowns, looked very attractive.
14. Sitting there every day, the old man almost became a landmark.
15. The children, frightened and crying, were huddled closely together.
16. Gliding smoothly over the water, our canoe soon reached the opposite shore.
17. The shrubs, bent by the almost constant wind, look like old men.
18. The tall tale told by the old trapper made us all laugh.
19. The old tower, leaning dangerously for years, has been torn down.
20. The tree, broken by the wind, was later uprooted.

Exercise 28: Infinitives, Gerunds, Participles— Part I

In the following sentences, (a) select the verbals and (b) tell whether each is a participle, gerund or infinitive. Use: P = participle, G = gerund, I = infinitive.

1. Packing oranges all day grows tiresome.
2. Everywhere we looked, we could see birds flying.
3. Driving at high speed, he tried to make the curve.

4. The cat would sit and wait for the coming of her mistress.

5. She likes to pick berries.
6. She ran down the stairs to greet her mother.
7. A barking dog stood on the porch.
8. The children began to sing.
9. Here is a book to read.
10. Swimming in the lake was his chief pastime.
11. Can you teach diving?
12. Opening the door, I saw two tramps.

13. The sun, peeping through the mist, cheered us greatly.

14. We watched the plane, twisting and turning in the air.

15. Our strawberries, planted last month, are doing very well.

16. My work is chiefly wrapping apples for shipment.

17. Shrieking loudly, he called our attention to his plight.

18. You must return the enclosed form.

19. Constant worrying made her very unhappy.

20. Wearied by playing, the puppy was soon asleep.

Exercise 29: Infinitives, Gerunds, Participles— Part II

In the following sentences, (a) select the verbals and (b) tell whether each is a participle, gerund or infinitive. Use: P = participle, G = gerund, I = infinitive.

1. Did you see a man coming down the street?

2. Our boat, rocking badly, seemed to be out of control.

3. The book being read was one we all liked.

4. Mother didn't approve of my buying a bike now.

5. With a pleased expression, he took his seat.

6. Swimming in salt water appealed to him.

7. You should keep your cancelled checks.

8. My cousin hopes to become an aviator.

9. To walk fast is difficult for some people.
10. Here is a house to rent.
11. Finally we could see the boy coming up the street.
12. Sitting in her room alone, Betty decided to write some poetry.
13. Calling loudly, the man ran from room to room.
14. We saw the parade coming, so we stopped to listen to the band.
15. Lying comfortably on the beach, we spent the day very enjoyably.
16. I am expected to write each week.
17. His doing little odd jobs brought him quite a bit of extra money.
18. Her part of the work is sweeping, while mine is dusting.
19. The dog, barking at the car, is Laddie.
20. The leaning palms made a very pretty sight.

12. Independent and Dependent Clauses

A **clause** is a part of a sentence and must contain a subject and a predicate.

A **principal** (or **independent**) **clause** expresses a complete thought when used by itself.

> We went for a walk after dinner.

A **subordinate** (or **dependent**) **clause** cannot be used alone to express a complete thought; it must be attached to a principal clause. (The subordinate clause in the following sentence is italicized.)

> We went for a walk *after we had finished our dinner.*

Exercise 30: Independent and Dependent Clauses—Part I

Arrange your answer paper in two columns as shown below. Indicate the *independent clauses* in the left column, the *dependent clauses* in the right column.

Independent Clauses   *Dependent Clauses*

1. He arrived just as the clock struck seven.
2. I will write in order that you know of our where-abouts.
3. As he entered the room, everyone cheered.
4. They laughed at the stories which were told.
5. Since you left, we have had beautiful weather.
6. Did you speak to the boy who looked so discour aged?
7. You should observe how I do this.
8. The reason why he left was never explained.
9. Whither thou goest, I will go.
10. If wishes were horses, we would all take a ride.
11. Is this the place where you left it?
12. The reason why he failed was not discussed.
13. No one can be happy who does not have a clear conscience.
14. From where I stood, I could see all.
15. I shall attend school until I am at least eighteen years old.
16. The shirt that he wore had been patched many times.

17. The man knocked on the door while shouting **my** name.
18. Before another day passes, you should call Fred.
19. By the time I arrived at the store, I had forgotten my errand.
20. While listening to the radio, she did her weekly mending.

Exercise 31: Independent and Dependent Clauses—Part II

Arrange your answer paper in two columns as shown below. Indicate the *independent clauses* in the left column, the *dependent clauses* in the right column.

Independent Clauses　　　　*Dependent Clauses*

1. Think twice before you answer.
2. As we drove through the country, we could see the results of the flood.
3. The lady who was at the door admitted us.
4. Will you please let me know when I should meet you?
5. They listened for the sound which was feared by all.
6. Always look before you leap.
7. The green house which stands on the hill is **my** home.

8. John Fields, who visited us last summer, is now at college

9. The book which I lost belongs to the library.

10. Before the storm reached its height, we were safely home.

11. The books lay where he had left them the night before.

12. Has anyone ever heard why he did not return?

13. I will bring the cake unless I forget it.

14. My father likes a steak which is cooked rare.

15. The puppy hid where we could not find her.

16. The problem was harder than I had realized.

17. When is a good time for me to call you?

18. After we had reached home, we built a warm fire and ate lunch.

19. Until the sun rose, we kept a guard at the gate.

20. We shall choose a day when you are all at home.

13. Adjective, Adverbial and Noun Clauses

Adjective clauses modify a noun or pronoun. They are introduced by: who, which, that, as little as, as many as, such as, as much as, wherein, where, etc.

The boy *who called me* is Tom Drake.
> (*who called me* is an adjective clause modifying the noun *boy*)

Adverbial clauses modify a verb, an adjective or an adverb. They are introduced by: when, where, before, since, if, while, after, as long as, because, that, whenever, although, though, so that, as, until, wherever, etc.

Mary cried *because she was scolded.*
> (*because she was scolded* is an adverbial clause modifying the verb *cried*)

They will be happy *if we visit them.*
> (*if we visit them* is an adverbial clause modifying the adjective *happy*)

Noun clauses are clauses used as nouns. They are introduced by: who, whom, which, what, that, whether, if (meaning whether), whose, where, how, when, why.

> *Why you did not get my letter* puzzles me.
> (*Why you did not get my letter* is a noun clause used as the subject of the sentence)

> I wonder *if she will come to the party.*
> (*if she will come to the party* is a noun clause used as object of the verb *wonder*)

> She couldn't see from *where she sat.*
> (*where she sat* is a noun clause used as the object of the preposition *from*)

The conjunction *that* is often omitted at the beginning of a noun clause.

> I hope *(that) we can find it.*

Exercise 32: Adjective, Adverbial and Noun Clauses—Part I

In the following sentences, *(a)* select the clauses and classify each as adjective, adverbial or noun, and *(b)* state its use in the sentence:

1. I saw them as they left the house.
2. This house, which has just been redecorated, belongs to Uncle John.
3. The principal said that he would not need us.
4. You must ask for what you do not see.

5. The kitten hid where the dog could not find her
6. How he can do it so well is really amazing.
7. As the plane flew by, everyone ran for shelter.
8. Yes, I will bring ice cream unless I forget it.
9. That he is not at fault is firmly believed by every-one.
10. People who quarrel are not pleasant companions.
11. Do you think she is sorry for what she said?
12. His strength is not equal to what he has to do.
13. I am sure he is now sorry for what he did.
14. They stopped to help the man who had engine trouble.
15. Bob lost all the money he had earned.
16. He saw too late that he had done the wrong lessons.
17. The pies that she baked were soon gone.
18. Because he had passed, he was very happy.
19. Since we are so late, we will not go in.
20. The dog listened intently, for he heard his master's voice.

Exercise 33: Adjective, Adverbial and Noun Clauses—Part II

In the following sentences, (a) select the clauses and classify each as adjective, adverbial or noun, and (b) state its use in the sentence:

1. His voice produced an effect
   I didn't like.

2. He asked if he might leave.
3. If you are quiet, you may sit here.
4. When he left, we all missed him.
5. Here is some candy that you will like.
6. This is a picture of Robert Frost, the poet who has
   written many poems about New England.
7. That he had won surprised everyone.
8. She found the book where she had left it.
9. Drink all the juice you want.
10. They robbed the house while we slept.
11. What they said did not matter much.
12. There may be some truth in what he has just said.
13. You will find it where you left it.
14. The boy was very sorry for what he had done.
15. Last night I dreamed I had a million dollars.
16. The book you are reading is mine.
17. We enjoyed all the places that we visited.
18. They will not go because it is raining.
19. After you have finished, give it to me.
20. Where he had been so long puzzled me.

14. *Restrictive and Non-Restrictive Clauses*

A **restrictive clause** is one which restricts or limits the statement made by the independent (or principal) clause and is necessary to complete the thought. In fact, the restrictive clause is so necessary to the independent clause that it is never separated from it by commas. It answers the questions: what kind? or which one?

> Weather *which is damp* makes me ill.
> > (*which is damp* is necessary to convey the correct meaning of the sentence; it is a *restrictive clause*)

A **non-restrictive clause** is one which does *not* restrict or limit the statement made in the independent (or principal) clause and is *not* necessary to complete the meaning of the sentence. Therefore, the non-restrictive clause is set off from the rest of the sentence by commas to show that it may be omitted without changing the correct meaning of the sentence.

Mr. Jones, *who lives next door,* is a doctor.

> (*who lives next door* is not necessary to convey the correct meaning of the sentence; it is a *non-restrictive clause*)

Exercise 34: Restrictive and Non-Restrictive Clauses

In each of the following sentences, *(a)* select the dependent clause and *(b)* tell whether it is restrictive (use R) or non-restrictive (use N). For the purpose of this exercise, commas, which set off a non-restrictive clause, have been intentionally omitted.

1. A house which is in need of paint looks unattractive.

2. The band which leads the procession won the state championship last year.

3. Water that is impure causes illness.
4. Philip who is an intelligent boy knew what to do in the emergency.

5. Father bought me a pony which had been brought from the West.

6. Franklin Roosevelt who was the thirty-first president of the United States was the first president to be elected for more than two consecutive terms.

7. Our crop which we planted in the valley will be entirely ruined if we get a heavy frost.

8. The girl who sang had a well-trained voice.

9. We bought an old car which was painted black.

10. Fruit which has spoiled is not good to eat.

11. Everyone who disobeys the laws should be punished.

12. Every boy and girl who does not study wastes time.

13. Our house which is a two-story building was damaged by fire.

14. Mrs. Brown who taught here last year is now a principal.

15. Mr. Smith who is a traveler has many interesting pictures.

16. I like the book that I am now reading.

17. New York which is the largest city in the United States has a population of seven million.

18. Ed Luna who lives next door has a young daughter.

19. I do not like a person who is untidy.

20. Don Jamison who now lives in California was my chum in college.

15. *Simple Subject and Predicate*

A **sentence** is a group of words expressing a complete thought. Every sentence must have a subject and a predicate. The subject and predicate may be simple or compound.

A **subject** is that of which something is said.

A **predicate** is that which is said about the subject.

A **simple subject** is composed of a noun or pronoun without any modifiers. A **compound subject** consists of two or more nouns or pronouns connected by a conjunction.

The *moon* was bright.

The *moon* and *stars* were bright.

In commands, the subject is (you) understood.

(You) Look at the sky.　　　*(You)* Pay attention.

A **simple predicate** is composed of a verb or verb phrase without any modifiers. A **compound predicate** consists of two or more verbs connected by a conjunction.

The man *sang* a song.　　　The man *sang* and *played.*

Exercise 35: Simple Subject and Predicate— Part I

Arrange your answer paper in two columns as shown below. Indicate the *subject words* in the left column, the *predicate words* in the right column.

Subject Words   *Predicate Words*

1. The sly old fox evaded all attempts at capture.

2. They felt happy after their success.
3. Can't you see them now?
4. Why did Mary not remain tonight?
5. The little boys and girls from our school sang and danced in a play for the benefit of the library.
6. Into the warm water plunged the eager children.
7. The boys on the raft could not be clearly seen from the shore.
8. Listen carefully to all directions.
9. Bring your books, paper and pencils to class tomorrow.

10. A large canning factory from New England has recently moved to a site near our city.
11. Books, papers and pencils lay all about.
12. They will get their diplomas in June.
13. To whom did you give the books?
14. The crowd was then told the facts of the case.
15. The old woman yelled and pounded upon the back door.
16. All of these stories will be enjoyed by adults and children.
17. During the night, many planes flew high over the mountains.
18. In 1540, fireworks were manufactured in Italy.
19. Sometimes children exhibit great courage in the face of danger.
20. Don't put them there.

Exercise 36: Simple Subject and Predicate— Part II

Arrange your answer paper in two columns as shown below. Indicate the *subject words* in the left column, the *predicate words* in the right column.

Subject Words   *Predicate Words*

1. No great book was ever written by her.
2. Into the road ran a boy and his dog.

3. My sister and I had a mis-
understanding.

4. Work hard and thoughtfully.
5. I have read these old books often.
6. Through the heavy fog, the little boat could not
be clearly seen.
7. To whom did you speak over the phone?
8. All of these books must be covered.
9. Mary and her brother went to school early today.
10. Come early, please.
11. With whom is she going?
12. Friends and family joined in the festivities.
13. In the Spring, we will go North.
14. The dogs barked and whined all evening.
15. Get up early.
16. Down the street dashed the frightened dog.
17. George is a musician and an artist.
18. Harry and Ed raced to the corner.
19. I awoke and raised the curtains.
20. During the afternoon, we had few customers.

16. Complete Subject and Predicate

The **complete subject** is the simple subject and all its modifiers.

The lonely old man on the corner came from the North.

The **complete predicate** is the simple predicate and all its modifiers.

The boys *ran rapidly down the hill.*

To find the complete subject and predicate in an inverted or in an interrogative sentence, change the word order into a statement; thus—

Into the valley of death rode the six hundred. (= The six hundred rode into the valley of death.)

Whose place are you taking? (= You are taking whose place.)

Exercise 37: Complete Subject and Predicate— Part I

Arrange your answer paper in two columns as shown below. Indicate the *complete subject* in the left column, the *complete predicate* in the right column.

    Complete Subject   *Complete Predicate*

1. Mother has finished my sweater.
2. Many huge sponges grow along the west coast of Florida.
3. In the hush of night a terrific explosion shook the town.
4. Why can't you come Wednesday?
5. Great was the force of the tornado.
6. On our farm there are four little puppies.
7. Do your aunt and uncle come here often?
8. Under no conditions would he give away the secret.
9. Go to the store for a bottle of milk and a loaf of bread.
10. Over and over turned the colorful kite.
11. The policeman and the angry man walked into the room.
12. Back and forth she walked, followed by the bewildered relatives.
13. Flat on their stomachs lay the frightened boys.
14. At last the day dawned bright and clear.

15. Did the girls meet in this room last night?
16. On the table was a picture of John.
17. In our garden many beautiful trees bloom throughout the year.
18. Could they not be a little quieter?
19. Why don't John and his brother attend this college?
20. Place the flowers on the table.

Exercise 38: Complete Subject and Predicate— Part II

Arrange your answer paper in two columns as shown below. Indicate the *complete subject* in the left column, the *complete predicate* in the right column.

Complete Subject   *Complete Predicate*

1. In front of the garage was parked a new car.
2. Father took Joe and me to the ballgame Saturday.
3. The old picture that hangs over the mantel is of great value.
4. Beyond the ridge of hills lay the quiet little town.
5. With whom did you go to the movies?
6. Take this to Miss Aldrich.
7. Hopefully the little child looked from face to face.
8. The boy who lives next door won the scholarship.
9. Finally we came to a gas station.
10. Under the desk lay my pen.

11. Seldom does she beat Helen at tennis.

12. At what time do you expect the train to arrive?
13. Sometimes she annoys us greatly.
14. This old car is certainly in need of repairs.
15. Why did you go without Harold?
16. The little dog that was lost has been found.
17. Into the water dived the happy youngsters.
18. Put it where no one will fall over it.
19. Shakespeare wrote many plays and sonnets.
20. Louder and louder grew the sound.

17. Simple, Compound and Complex Sentences

Sentences are classified according to form as simple, compound and complex.

A **simple sentence** has only one subject and one predicate, either or both of which may be compound.

> It was a beautiful day.
> The days and nights were cool.
> The children danced and sang.

A **compound sentence** has two or more principal (or independent) clauses.

> The boys played outdoor games, and their fathers decided to join them just for fun.
> You are wrong; hence, you must admit it.

A **complex sentence** has one principal (or independent) clause and one or more dependent (or subordinate) clauses. (The dependent clauses in the following sentences are italicized.)

> The boy *who sang* is from Chicago.
> *If you watch closely,* you will see how he does it.

Exercise 39: Simple, Compound and Complex Sentences—Part I

Classify the following sentences as *simple* (use S), *compound* (use Cd) or *complex* (use Cx):

1. Last year was one which I should like to live again.
2. The days and nights were very pleasant.
3. The wind had abated and we could see destruction all about.
4. If you do not complete the work, you must not leave early.
5. This is the house that I mean.
6. Bananas that are green are not ripe for eating.
7. The dog sprang upon the burglar.
8. When we last saw him, he was with Bill.
9. It is a very interesting book.
10. The boy who lost his coat is Herbert.
11. Everyone wanted the party, but no one would accept the responsibility.
12. The children played all day.
13. Think of America in 1776 and think of America today.
14. It is an interesting letter; it should be read by every parent.
15. Though I had seen the picture, I could not remember the title.
16. They saw the land and shouted for joy.

17. When they saw the land, they shouted for joy.
18. The boys whom you saw do not live here.
19. I do not know the reason why he is absent.
20. The stream where he fishes is miles from the city.

Exercise 40: Simple, Compound and Complex Sentences—Part II

Classify the following sentences as *simple* (use S), *compound* (use Cd) or *complex* (use Cx):

1. Joan, Bob and Henry ran all the way to school.
2. I have often wished that some day I will be rich.
3. When the bell rings, take your seats quietly.
4. John walked to school, but Mary rode with her mother.
5. We signaled to the men, but they did not stop.
6. The skates which I saw were on sale at the Bargain Shop.
7. We left the key where Billy would find it.
8. I thought you went directly home after school.
9. The flowers were carefully planted, yet they never grew well.
10. I shouted while he waved the flag.
11. The man who called is an old friend of mine.
12. Henry is a good swimmer and goes to the beach every weekend.
13. You must come when I call.

14. We picked up the dog which was shivering with the cold.

15. When they called, I was not yet up.

16. He could not make up his mind; he just sat and looked very unhappy.

17. The child hid where we could not find her.

18. He caught a fish and shouted for joy.

19. As soon as you have finished, bring your work to me.

20. Though I am tired, I shall gladly go with you.

Exercise 41: Simple, Compound and Complex Sentences—Part III

Classify the following sentences as *simple* (use S), *compound* (use Cd) or *complex* (use Cx):

1. Since I had not made reservations, I did not expect to get a room.

2. He rapped on the door, but no one answered his call.

3. He wrote to us many times while he was away.

4. While the orchestra played, I tried to remember my speech.

5. The students and their parents came in great numbers.

6. We had to drink our coffee black, since we had forgotten the cream.

7. I saw monkeys, eagles and sea-lions at the zoo.

8. They had intended to stay only a short time, but they remained all evening.

9. As the sun rose, we crept out of bed.

10. Although he was very angry, he held his tongue.

11. The trees which grow here were planted by my mother.

12. You are a true friend; you always help me.

13. An actor who had become famous bought our home.

14. When Dad came home, we had dinner.

15. I quickly put out the light and jumped into bed.

16. The door sagged and the roof leaked badly.

17. He runs, jumps and plays all kinds of games.

18. This is the one that I mean.

19. I expect to pass the test, yet I am not too confident.

20. Put this money where you will not lose it.

18. *Declarative, Interrogative, Imperative and Exclamatory Sentences*

Sentences are classified according to use as declarative, interrogative, imperative and exclamatory.

A **declarative sentence** makes a statement.

We took a long walk.

An **interrogative sentence** asks a question.

Where is Mary?

An **imperative sentence** expresses a command.

Take your hat off.

An **exclamatory sentence** expresses strong or sudden feeling.

My, how cold it was today!

Exercise 42: Declarative, Interrogative, Imperative and Exclamatory Sentences—Part I

Classify the following sentences as *declarative* (use Dec.), *interrogative* (use Int.), *imperative* (use Imp.) or *exclamatory* (use Ex.):

1. Look, there it is now!
2. The birds flew about.
3. How many boxes of eggs did you sell?
4. Give me liberty or give me death!
5. How beautiful it is!
6. Throw that away at once.
7. Jane was amused at the performance.
8. On warm days we go swimming.
9. What does he want?
10. Put it there on the chair.
11. Oh, how hot it is!
12. Name the capital of your state.
13. When are you going to Aunt Ann's again?
14. We have to cross a bridge when we go to Canada.
15. Washington worshipped at St. Paul's Church when he was in New York.
16. Why don't you know?
17. Three cheers for our men!
18. His cold is much better now.
19. Put six in each box.
20. Why didn't you answer?

Exercise 43: Declarative, Interrogative, Imperative and Exclamatory Sentences—Part II

Classify the following sentences as *declarative* (use Dec.), *interrogative* (use Int.), *imperative* (use Imp.) or *exclamatory* (use Ex.):

1. Close the door.
2. Where are your books?
3. This bread is not fresh.
4. Hurrah! He made it!
5. Please put them there.
6. Everyone had gone by then.
7. Leave your books on your desk.
8. When you get back, sit down and study.
9. This is the store where I bought my watch.
10. Did you take pictures of Niagara Falls?
11. She seems to like history.
12. What a wonderful time we should have!
13. Have you seen Ed today?
14. I like this new book very much.
15. This is the one I mean.
16. What a game it was!
17. Are you going to the movies with Ann?
18. When did Father arrive?
19. We took several pictures, but none came out very well.
20. Please go to the store for me.

19. *Incomplete and Run-On Sentences*

An **incomplete sentence** lacks a subject, a predicate or both. Do *not* punctuate a phrase or dependent clause as a separate sentence; attach it to a main clause.

Incomplete: Holding the bundle tightly . . .
　　　　　　(lacks a subject)
Complete:　He held the bundle tightly.

Incomplete: My friend Tom Brown . . .
　　　　　　(lacks a predicate)
Complete:　My friend Tom Brown moved to another city.

Incomplete: When he didn't return . . .
　　　　　　(lacks a main clause)
Complete:　When he didn't return, I called the office.

A **run-on sentence** consists of two or more sentences written as one. To correct this error, divide the sentence into two separate sentences; or insert a subordinate conjunction; or punctuate by means of a semicolon.

Run-on: You must be very careful the road is rough.

Correct: You must be very careful. The road is rough.
(formed two sentences)

Correct: You must be very careful because the road is rough.
(inserted the subordinate conjunction *because*)

Correct: You must be very careful; the road is rough.
(punctuated with a semicolon)

Exercise 44: Incomplete and Run-On Sentences —Part I

Rewrite whichever groups of words are incomplete or run-on expressions. Some are correct and complete as they stand; mark these "correct."

1. After the cool winter weather.
2. Finally the joyful day arrived.
3. This is delicious ice cream where did you buy it?
4. Hold your club this way, or you will tear up the green.
5. You may not like spinach however it is good for you.
6. What time is it I haven't eaten yet I am very hungry.
7. Pupils having to purchase new supplies.

8. An orange tree and a vine.
9. Behind the old shed where much lumber was piled.
10. Put the tea here I may want some more.
11. I have a new book, it is interesting and humorous.
12. Because their telephone is out of order.
13. The beach was crowded with tourists and natives.
14. The leaves falling from the tree.
15. When the dawn came at last.
16. Bob wants you to help him, can you?
17. When I returned yesterday, I found my friends waiting for me.
18. The waves dashed endlessly on the beach.
19. Rex, our long-lost dog.
20. Pitching and tossing on the ocean at night.

Exercise 45: Incomplete and Run-On Sentences —Part II

Rewrite whichever groups of words are incomplete or run-on expressions. Some are correct and complete as they stand; mark these "correct."

1. The driver with his hand on the emergency brake.
2. At the close of a very exciting day.
3. Don't make fun of him, he doesn't know any better.
4. I can't help you now you will have to return later.
5. Those cold December days having so quickly passed.
6. Cricket, an English game, is very similar to our baseball.

7. Tired and dirty after our long ride.
8. Quickly he responded to the call of his friends.
9. Because he felt like it.
10. I'll take this one, it attracts me.
11. Although I don't really believe you did it.
12. In our town is a large vacant field where we played ball all summer.
13. The flag flying in the breeze.
14. Riding in a fast boat.
15. They placed the oars in the boat.
16. Into the old house about midnight.
17. Steve can come with me I enjoy his company.
18. Don't wait for me, I may be very late.
19. Spending many happy hours at the seashore.
20. He was approaching me when the bell rang.

Exercise 46: Incomplete and Run-On Sentences —Part III

Rewrite whichever groups of words are incomplete or run-on expressions. Some are correct and complete as they stand; mark these "correct."

1. When I reached their home, the lights were out I went home.
2. The day before Christmas was one of great preparation.
3. Into the old deserted house without flashlight or gun.

4. At the end of the day.
5. Isn't this fine it is just what I wanted.
6. Over the radio came my favorite song.
7. Swinging widely around the dangerous corner.
8. Sliding down the slippery path.
9. I went home early I helped get dinner then I read for a while.
10. Because he had not finished.
11. They found the child and started for home.
12. A boy with large brown eyes.
13. At the close of the most interesting day in my life.
14. Be quiet, I can't hear the program.
15. The window was suddenly shattered.
16. At last the letter came.
17. Just as we ran into the shop.
18. I have a new dog, it is a terrier and very intelligent.
19. When we left home.
20. I returned in September, fully rested and ready for work.

Exercise 47: Incomplete and Run-On Sentences —Part IV

Rewrite whichever groups of words are incomplete or run-on expressions. Some are correct and complete as they stand; mark these "correct."

1. The man on the corner.
2. Yesterday he was ill today he feels much better.

3. Down the lonely road at a quick pace.
4. There was a light in the distance; it flashed on and off.
5. Who spoke to you yesterday?
6. We arrived there at last we could find no place to stay.
7. Though you will be excused early.
8. At last the task was finished.
9. Sarah has practiced this piece for weeks, she is to play it in the assembly.
10. The window slammed shut.
11. The old piece of china on the mantel, a priceless gift from Aunt Mary.
12. Louder and louder sounded the thunder.
13. What's the matter can't you find your homework?
14. Many visitors come here each year, some have been coming for years.
15. Hanging frantically to the old canoe.
16. At last he had reached the shore.
17. The little birds sitting on the branch of the tree.
18. An old man with a small boy.
19. Our team has won every game, we feel that they have done well.
20. Aunt Martha fully ready for any emergency.

20. *Misplaced Modifiers*

In a sentence the modifying word, phrase or clause should come as near to the word it modifies as possible. If the modifier is misplaced, the sentence often sounds absurd, or the meaning becomes obscured. To correct the error, rewrite the sentence by shifting the modifier or by inserting the words required by the meaning.

Wrong: A piano is wanted by a lady with three wooden legs.

Right: A piano with three wooden legs is wanted by a lady.

(In the *wrong* sentence, the phrase *with three wooden legs* modifies *lady,* but in the *right* sentence it modifies *piano.*)

Wrong: Coming around the corner, my house is the first on the left.

Right: Coming around the corner, you will find my house is the first on the left.

(In the *wrong* sentence, the person spoken to is not mentioned. It appears that *house* will be coming around the

corner, whereas in the *right* sentence it
is *you*.)

Exercise 48: Misplaced Modifiers

Rewrite the following sentences, putting the misplaced
modifiers in the correct position, or inserting the words
required by the meaning:

1. I saw a snake going to our class picnic.
2. Flying around the room, I saw two bats.
3. A very invigorating exercise, I like swimming.
4. A horse is wanted by a man weighing about 1500
   pounds and saddle-broken.
5. They hardly noticed the old man, enjoying an exciting game of hide-and-seek.
6. Eating the mouse, the child intently watched the
   kitten.
7. Baking bread, Edith, my baby sister, watched every
   move Mother made.
8. He put his lunch in his pocket which he ate later
   so that he would not forget it.
9. While eating my dinner, a cat came to the door.

10. He always takes along a
    bag of peanuts in his brief-
    case which he feeds to the
    elephants.

11. Walking along the road, a fire was discovered.
12. Ralph caught a glimpse of the parade standing on the chair.
13. To be cooked right, the pan must be very hot before the meat is put in.
14. Coming in on the bus, our new high school was seen.
15. Hurrying to get to school, my shoe came off at the corner.

16. Being only eight, my mother says that I am too young to go so far alone.

17. Entering the library, books are seen on display all about.
18. Coming up the lane, a huge tree confronted me.
19. The old horse fell into an open well on its back.
20. Being a savage dog, Aunt Polly was very cautious when she approached the house.

21. *Parallel Structure*

Parallel structure means that two or more ideas in a sentence are expressed in similar form; that is, in parallel grammatical elements. *And, but* and *or* usually join like terms—two nouns, two adjectives, two verbs, two adverbs, two phrases, two clauses, etc.

Wrong: Joe likes *boxing* and *to hike.*
   (*boxing* is a gerund, *to hike* is an infinitive)

Right: Joe likes *boxing* and *hiking.*
   (two gerunds)

Right: Joe likes *to box* and *to hike.*
   (two infinitives)

Wrong: She is *beautiful, intelligent* and *has charm.*
   (*beautiful* and *intelligent* are adjectives; *charm* is a noun)

Right: She is *beautiful, intelligent* and *charming.*
   (three adjectives)

Exercise 49: Parallel Structure

Rewrite the following sentences so that they are parallel in structure:

1. Write a theme with a good plot and which has at least a hundred words.
2. Mr. Jones has promised me a good position and to pay me a fair salary.
3. Some people seemed to care and others indifferent.
4. They left at once and rapidly.
5. My ambition is to be a doctor and specializing in surgery.
6. The Mayor asked both parties to meet and discuss their differences and finally arriving at a compromise.
7. The newspaper contains news, pictures, ads, tells you where to shop, and feature columns.
8. Table tennis, soap modeling, or to read mystery stories took up most of his spare time.
9. She likes to sit and chat, but I prefer doing things.
10. This is the life—to live, working and cooking outdoors.
11. We will get some things for cash but the rest on the payment of specified amounts at certain times.
12. Clean up, paint up, brightening the home each spring.
13. She is studious hardworking, and never gives up trying.

14. Running to base, he slipped, got up, and was keeping on going as fast as he could.

15. Let's go down to the cafeteria for a sandwich, cake, and drinking some milk or fruit juice.

16. After hard work at the office and he travels a long way home, Dad deserves a little rest.

17. The outer covering of the flesh, tissue, bone, and muscle need more than blood circulation for continuing life.

18. Raking the leaves, burning them, or to leave them on the ground till the snow comes marks the end of autumn.

19. Will you please close the door, take your seat, and do you mind finishing your work?

20. We tried to snap pictures and catch fish, but we got mosquito bites and sunburned.

22. Punctuation

Use the period:

1. After declarative and imperative sentences.

> It was a long day.   Close the door.

> The polite request as a question should be followed by a period instead of by a question mark.

> Will you please send me your latest catalog.

2. After abbreviations.

> Ill. (Illinois), Jan. (January), Dr. (Doctor)

3. After initials.

> R. L. Jones (Robert Louis Jones)

> Do not use a period after a part of a name used as a whole.

> Rob (Robert) didn't hear me.

Use the comma:

1. To separate from the rest of the sentence a word used in direct address.

> Close the door, Jane.
> Yes, Fred, it is true.

2. To separate an appositive word, phrase or clause from the rest of the sentence.

> Mr. Jones, our neighbor, is away.

> Mary, the girl who sang, is my cousin.

Do not set off by commas words that are closely related in meaning.

> I saw your brother Tony.

> My uncle Dave is visiting us.

3. To separate a series of words or expressions.

> Get some meat, bread and sugar.
> > *or:*
> Get some meat, bread, and sugar.

4. To separate a direct quotation from the rest of the sentence.

> "This," he said, "is where I live."

> "This is where I live," he said.

5. To separate the clauses of a long compound sentence.

> She did not reply, nor did I suggest an answer.

6. To separate a long dependent clause from the independent clause in a complex sentence if the dependent clause comes first.

If you make up your mind to try hard, you will succeed.

but:

You will succeed if you make up your mind to try hard.

7. To separate *yes, no* and *well* from the sentence or statement which follows them.

Yes, I see it now.   No, you may not.

8. To separate the day of the month from the year.

July 6, 1946   Monday, January 10, 1946

9. To separate a contrasting expression which is introduced by *not . . . but, not only . . . but also.*

Mary will be graduated, not in January, but in June.

10. To set off words, phrases and clauses which are out of their natural order.

The boys, wet and tired, sat down to rest.

Seated in his chair, Father settled all world problems.

11. To set off a non-restrictive clause.

James, who is our cousin, was the hero of the game.

12. To set off transitional words and phrases.

> Henry, of course, should also go.

> On the other hand, I didn't have the money to spend.

13. To separate the name of the city from the name of the state or country.

> Miami, Florida   London, England

14. After the complimentary close of a letter.

> Sincerely yours,   Your friend,

15. After the salutation (greeting) of a friendly letter.

> Dear Joe,   Dear Mary,

16. To indicate the omission of a word.

> I like candy; Jim, ice cream. (= Jim *likes* ice cream)

Use the colon:

1. After the salutation (greeting) of a business letter.

> Dear Sir: Gentlemen:

2. Before a list of particulars, an illustration or a statement.

> I went to the movies three times this week: Monday, Wednesday, and Friday.

3. In time expressions.

    6:10   7:25   8:40

Use the semicolon:

1. To separate the clauses of a compound sentence when no conjunction is used or when one of the clauses contains commas.

   I must leave now; I am expected home.

   I saw boats, tanks and automobiles; but the huge planes were not there.

2. Between the clauses of a compound sentence that are joined by also, so, thus, however, then, hence, otherwise, still, besides, nevertheless, accordingly.

   You have worked hard; therefore, you may have a vacation.

3. Usually before *thus, namely* and *as* where used to introduce examples.

   Four people were spoken of; namely, Jane, Fred, Jerry and Dan.

Use the question mark:

1. After an interrogative sentence.

   Why did you leave?

2. Within a parenthesis to express uncertainty.

   The date was January 15 (?), 1945.

Use the exclamation mark:

1. After a word, sound, group of words or a sentence that expresses surprise, sudden grief or joy, or some other strong feeling.

   Look! There is the new car!

   Ouch! That hurt!

Use quotation marks:

1. To enclose a direct quotation and each part of a broken (divided) quotation.

   She said, "I do not like it."

   "This is the one," she said, "that I do not like."

   Quotation marks are not used in the indirect quotation.

   She said that she did not like it.

2. A quotation within a quotation is set off by single quotation marks.

   Mother said to me, "John shouted, 'I will not do it!' "

To distinguish a word or letter which is to be discussed. (In printing, italics may be used.)

Use the word "frequent" in a sentence.

4. A quotation which is several paragraphs long should have quotation marks at the beginning of each paragraph and at the end of the last paragraph.

. To indicate the titles of books, poems, articles, etc., and for the names of ships, etc.

"Treasure Island"   "Fog"   "Queen Mary"

Use parentheses:

1. To show that the part enclosed within them is merely for explanation.

If we have a vacation at Christmas (and I know we will), I will visit you.

Use the dash:

1. To show a sudden change in thought or in construction.

I am planning to go—but why should I tell you?

2. To join an uninterrupted series of numbers.

1940—1950   Chapters V—X

Use the apostrophe:

1. To form the possessive case of nouns and indefinite pronouns.

   Helen's coat   one's self

2. To form the plural of numbers and letters

   4's   A's

3. To show the omission of letters or numbers.

   don't   Gov't   o'clock   class of '42

   Caution: Possessive pronouns *never* take an apostrophe: its, hers, ours, theirs

Use the hyphen:

1. When it is necessary to divide a word at the end of a line. The division should be made between syllables, and the hyphen should come at the end of the line.

   Example: intro-
             duction

2. In writing compound nouns.

   sister-in-law, commander-in-chief, attorney-at-law

3. To join words combined into a single adjective.

   a well-to-do man, a happy-go-lucky person

4. In compound numbers from twenty-one to ninety-nine and in fractions.

Twenty-two is one-quarter of eighty-eight.

Exercise 50: Using the Comma—Part I

Using the *comma* properly, punctuate the following sentences:

1. Here Mother is a note from Mr. Banker our principal.
2. Babs Jane and Mary will be there Mother.
3. They got here February 16 1945.
4. "That" he said "is a matter of great importance."
5. No these are not for sale.
6. Well Dick why don't you know?
7. Yes if you must know I am he.
8. Here is my new friend Bob Jones.
9. Florida my home state is very dear to me.
10. "This" she said "is my final decision."
11. In order to get there on time I arose at six.
12. I'd like you to meet Mr. and Mrs. Marks our new neighbors.
13. There were oranges tangerines and grapefruit for sale.
14. You may if you aren't too particular ride in the truck.
15. May we send boxes Mrs. Babbitt filled with candy oranges and nuts?

16. This you may be sure will give you excellent instruction.
17. John said "Well Fred will you believe it now?"
18. You will find no doubt that I am right.
19. The days and nights were warm and sunny but the flies and mosquitos were unbearable.
20. Send my letters Mother to 463 Rogers Street Brooklyn New York.

Exercise 51: Using the Comma—Part II

Using the *comma* properly, punctuate the following sentences:

1. I called on Mr. Young our new teacher.
2. When you go home will you please stop for me?
3. "It was yesterday" she said.
4. This Geraldine is what I mean.
5. Leave it here Walter.
6. By the time we get there it will be too late.
7. You have decided then that you will leave school?
8. Tom doesn't like olives Fred.
9. He did not reply nor did he show any interest.
10. No you may not go.
11. Here is Boston my birthplace.
12. Boys please be quiet.
13. Have you ever been in Washington D.C.?
14. Whom do you expect Uncle Joe?

15. She has in fact never been late.
16. The painting a beautiful rural scene was purchased for fifty dollars.

17. Let me illustrate Sam what really happened.

18. Well where are you?
19. Ralph was born on Monday February 10 1946.
20. On Saturday said Martin let's go to the library together.

Exercise 52: Punctuation—Part I

Punctuate correctly the following sentences:

1. How she asked did you know
2. Did you see this Mary
3. Mr J L Jones is from Chicago Ill
4. Dr Frederick was away from Nov 6 1945 until Feb 11 1946
5. Well John did you win

6. Rover our little dog jumped over the fence

7. They live at 145 Melrose Avenue St Petersburg Florida
8. Ben the captain of our team is an honor student
9. What do you want James inquired
10. Mr Franks where are you
11. Bring some bread butter and sugar
12. Four boys were mentioned namely Bill Fred George and Jack
13. Please close the window Henry
14. Jim likes swimming Arthur baseball
15. This is therefore your last chance
16. They drove from Toledo Ohio to Ft Wayne Indiana
17. Well if you must know it is mine
18. Why dont you cross your ts and make your as more plainly
19. When Pat called she found me very busy
20. Where he asked are you

Exercise 53: Punctuation—Part II

Punctuate correctly the following sentences:

1. I dont want it she cried
2. Hurrah There he is now
3. The painting a mass of colors did not appeal to me
4. Betty Ellen and George arrived on time
5. No the man isnt here
6. I hope Bob said that I may go too

7. Dont make your 7s look like 9s
8. The night cool and clear made us unwilling to go home
9. Bring the following books papers and maps
10. The salesmans samples included mens suits
11. He said Where are you
12. Where he said are you
13. Where are you he said
14. To make so many mistakes is bad enough but not to correct them is worse
15. You have been told often Frank yet you dont seem to understand
16. My what a day
17. Whos at the door Frances
18. Give it to Florence the girl in the front seat
19. We dont usually need heavy clothing here but this year we surely do
20. I was so frightened Mary admitted when I yelled I did it

Exercise 54: Punctuation—Part III

Punctuate correctly the following sentences:

1. The tall erect man inquired Where is the City Hall
2. No you will never know
3. He bought several kinds of fruit oranges tangerines and bananas
4. What is the dogs name Mary

5. George why didnt you write your theme
6. It was a beautiful May day we went on a picnic
7. The next day was cool therefore we remained at home
8. We saw alligators tarpon and seagulls but we didnt catch a thing
9. They launched the Lexington a new ship
10. Cant you do Mothers dishes for her Bobby
11. We leave now shouted the boys
12. The singer arrived late I was informed and on her arrival they found she was very ill
13. When it rains we always remain indoors
14. The stranger asked where the theater is
15. The vacation was planned for Tuesday July 8 1946
16. Well Freddie where is it
17. The work was very difficult however I did get some pleasure from doing it
18. Didnt they once live in Galveston Texas
19. Bill the tall boy in the rear stood up
20. Marys books are lost arent they

Exercise 55: Punctuation—Part IV

Punctuate correctly the following *direct* and *indirect* *quotations:*

1. Where are your books Mrs Black inquired
2. My brother asked me where I had left his gloves

3. The game will begin at eight oclock said the coach
4. The coach said that the game would begin at eight oclock
5. Are you going to the game asked Jerry
6. Yes said Mother
7. I think suggested Father that you had better study for an hour
8. He answered I will see you Monday
9. Where is my ink asked Betty
10. He answered that he was tired
11. John said I am very sorry
12. Well Mother said where were you
13. Well Fred said his mother I am not sure
14. This is the one Miss Jones answered the reporter
15. She kept asking me why I had been late yesterday
16. Why dont you leave she asked
17. She asked why he didnt leave
18. Father said he would meet them
19. Father replied I will meet them
20. He asked where he should leave them

23. Capitalization

Capitalize:

1. The first word of every sentence.
2. The first word of every line of poetry.
3. The first word of every direct quotation.

   He replied, "No, I did not see Fred."

4. Proper nouns and proper adjectives.

   Atlanta   Spanish

5. The names of the days of the week, months of the year and holidays.

   Sunday, May, Fourth of July

6. The beginning of every word of a person's name, and initials.

   Jack Frederick Johnson

   J. F. Johnson

7. Names referring to the Deity or sacred books· Old Testament, the Bible, Psalms, the Almighty.

8. Titles and the abbreviations of titles.

   Father Jones   Dr. Joe Frink

   Sir William Brown   Sgt. Fred Wall

   A title referring to a particular person is also capitalized.

   The President of Brazil is in America.

   I will go with Mother.

9. Geographical places, important buildings and historical events.

   the South, Empire State Building, the Battle of Bunker Hill

10. In the titles of books, themes, poems, stories and essays, the first word and all other words except articles, short prepositions and conjunctions.

    "The Last of the Mohicans" (novel)

    "The Lady of the Lake" (poem)

    "The Fall of the House of Usher" (story)

    "On Unanswering Letters" (essay)

11. In the names of political parties, stores, churches, events, wars and theaters, the first word and all other words except articles, short prepositions and conjunctions.

St. Mary's Church	United Nations
Radio City Theater	Carnegie Hall
The Great Atlantic & Pacific Tea Co.	Metropolitan Museum of Art

12. The words North, East, South and West when they are used to refer to sections of the country.

> We went North last summer.

13. The words O and I.

14. The first word and the principal word in the salutation of a friendly letter.

> Dear John,   My dear Friend,

15. The nouns park, company, river, lake, society, mountain, street, club, avenue, hotel, school, etc., when they are used as a part of a particular name.

> Lake Erie, Rocky Mountains, Yellowstone National Park, Hudson River, Pacific Ocean, Lotos Club

Exercise 56: Capitalization—Part I

pitalize the following sentences:

1. we crossed the mississippi river three times.
2. the jamison company is having a sale.
3. we swim every sunday in the gulf of mexico.

4. providence street is the longest street in our city.
5. last night i met lieutenant franklin.
6. "my history paper is lost," said jane.
7. we listened with interest to sir james brown.
8. i listened while he read a passage from the bible.
9. the adirondack mountains are in new york state.
10. the all state club meets every monday.
11. his theme was entitled "the rights and wrongs done each day."
12. have you read "the trail of the lonesome pine"?
13. last night we listened to the president of the united states.
14. our neighbor, mr. crane, once lived in the west.
15. latin is as difficult as mathematics.
16. last week we studied the poem "on the road to vagabondia."
17. the hudson river lay before us.
18. have you ever seen the statue of liberty?
19. give the report to dr. harold j. evans.
20. i went north with mother and father last june.

Exercise 57: Capitalization—Part II

Capitalize the following sentences:

1. last july we took a trip through the southwest.
2. patrick henry said, "give me liberty or give me death."
3. noah is a biblical name.

4. can you read a french newspaper?
5. jane went there last year with father.
6. i once lived in coral gables, fla.
7. my aunt attended a meeting of the red cross.
8. we camped at clear lake.
9. "here," said bill, "is my english paper."
10. mr. jones is a republican.
11. i went to chicago with mother.
12. everyone should serve the lord.
13. will you attend the colburn school next year?
14. i like uncle sam better than any other uncle of mine.
15. john could not go with his mother.
16. does grand avenue have a traffic light?
17. we read a mystery entitled "the case of the howling dog."
18. if you attend college next year, will it be rollins college at winter park?
19. each afternoon we swim at the royal palm hotel.
20. i lost my latin and biology books.

Exercise 58: Capitalization—Part III

Capitalize the following sentences:

1. i shall return sunday, november 6.
2. he asked, "why did you leave?"
3. do you live on second avenue?
4. mr. w. e. gladstone will arrive friday.

5. he wrote a theme about admiral dewey.
6. the pacific ocean is west of us.
7. all the men attended a rally given by the democratic party.
8. we invited father duffy to attend our party on new year's day.
9. the como quick lunch is a small restaurant on our street.
10. i heard dad say, "pick up your gloves."
11. the title of the article is "a year in the open."
12. i received a new bible from aunt marge.
13. i am studying english, chemistry, history and spanish.
14. we are all glad to be here in the united states of america.
15. we have always lived in the east.
16. new orleans is south of us.
17. the strand theater is the largest theater in our city.
18. the crestview school is in belleview park.
19. the junior red cross invited mrs. adams to speak.
20. the fourth of july is on sunday.

Exercise 59: Punctuation and Capitalization— Part I

Rewrite the following sentences, *punctuating* and *capitalizing* them correctly:

1. get some bread meat and sugar

2. well marian close the door
3. there he said is where i live
4. where were you july 6 1945
5. mrs w l jacobs is our english teacher
6. miss flora s smith was my french teacher last year
7. the day warm and humid made us perspire
8. all at once he said now i know the answer mr brown
9. his greatest fault is but whats the use of discussing that again
10. where is florences bicycle teresa
11. what shall i do the car wont start he exclaimed
12. yes you may go now said joe at last
13. this is very useful it saves much time
14. its not ready yet jane
15. are these as good as marys john
16. mr lawrence my brothers friend is an artist
17. jane lives in miami jerry in tampa
18. i have just finished reading the red badge of courage
19. the pilgrims wanted to worship god as they please
20. cant we do some of mothers work for her sue

Exercise 60: Punctuation and Capitalization— Part II

Rewrite the following sentences, *punctuating* and *capitalizing* them correctly:

1. is your cottage near the pacific ocean

2. you should be able to help yourself nevertheless i will help you
3. there said jim is john my cousin
4. mary said quietly i am sure no one has touched it
5. his name is robert 1 jones said mary and he is in our class dont forget to invite him
6. on july 14 the french celebrate bastille day
7. are the democrats and republicans planning their campaigns
8. i learned to speak the italian and french languages
9. does he take the times and the tribune
10. well aunt maude did you really win this time
11. yes mr jiggs said the voice over the telephone i am professor james but i think you want to speak to the head of the department
12. why dont you try the contest perhaps youll win
13. did you study english and history under mr brown
14. last year we went to the mountains this year to the seashore
15. at last we found what do you think
16. while walking along fourth street with louise we met florence
17. this is bad boys said mr mills what are you going to do about it
18. labor day always comes on monday
19. no ken isnt here yet
20. why do you ask so many questions dad complained

Exercise 61: Punctuation and Capitalization— Part III

Rewrite the following sentences, *punctuating* and *capitalizing* them correctly:

1. this lesson sam isnt too difficult
2. oh what a scare you gave me
3. these books i assure you are a bargain
4. there is however a better road
5. please bring the following eggs salad and cake
6. while playing tennis with freda i hurt my leg
7. where were you she demanded
8. we taught her the star spangled banner
9. i am going to write a composition on how to make model planes
10. we left tuesday february 18 for cleveland ohio
11. the farmer sold corn oats potatoes and wheat
12. tell me doctor lewis are you going to lecture today
13. lets join the y m c a norman
14. i was given this new bible by father kelly
15. yes mary you may go but dont stay out too late
16. wait for me the girl said
17. the girl said wait for me
18. wait the girl said until i arrive
19. frank entered the race but he didnt win
20. we went to the paramount theater on saturday and on sunday we went to uncle freds house

24. The Direct Object

The **direct object** (object of the verb) is a noun o. pronoun in the predicate which denotes the receiver or the result of the action of the verb.

Father bought a new *car*.　　Yesterday I saw *him*.

To locate the direct object, ask yourself: *"Who or what* received the action of the verb?" In the first sentence, *car* answers the question *"What* did my father buy?" In the second sentence, *him* answers the question *"Whom* did you see yesterday?"

Exercise 62: The Direct Object—Part I

Select the *direct objects* in the following sentences:

1. The teacher sounded the gong.
2. Mike shined Mr. Brown's shoes for him.
3. Mary called me over the phone.
4. They were studying electricity in their science class.
5. The children were learning grammar.
6. Mother drove the car into town.

7. All the children waved tiny flags.
8. The lightning demolished the house and garage.
9. We heard the angry cry of the mountain lion.
10. The hunter shot the deer.
11. The automobile struck the careless child.
12. Someone has destroyed the fence.
13. Who will inherit his large estate?
14. On her return trip, she visited us.
15. The principal read some verses from the Bible at assembly.
16. Have you returned the books?

17. The first shot wounded the lion.

18. I wrote four themes for my English class.
19. Mother has finished her dress.
20. The teacher assigned a long lesson for Thursday

Exercise 63: The Direct Object—Part II

Select the *direct objects* in the following sentences:

1. He rode the horse into the swirling stream.

2. She evidently did not understand you.
3. Dan chased the dog for miles.
4. Last spring we bought a new boat.
5. Did you write a letter to your sister?
6. He kicked the ball through the window.
7. Please sharpen my pencil.
8. I suppose she didn't hear me.
9. I bought some peas, carrots and turnips at the market.
10. I shall not answer such foolish questions.
11. Bring paper, pen and ink to class tomorrow.
12. We played four games last week.
13. The old dog buried a bone in the sand.
14. Probably you passed him on the avenue.
15. We saw many gulls on the bridge.
16. Father bought new gloves, shoes and socks yesterday.
17. Would you sing a song in chapel?
18. The boys built a shack by the river.
19. Mother has knit seven sweaters since November.
20. Didn't you see her yesterday?

25. The Indirect Object

The **indirect object** is a noun or pronoun which shows to whom or for whom, to what or for what, the action of the verb is directed. Three ways of testing for an indirect object are:

1. The indirect object must come between the direct object and the verb.

2. You can put the prepositions *to* or *for* before the indirect object without changing the meaning of the sentence.

3. To have an indirect object, there must always be a direct object.

> Dad bought (for) *Tom* a new *suit.*
>
> > (*Tom* is the indirect object; *suit* is the direct object)
>
> Mother gave (to) *him* a *ring.*
>
> > (*him* is the indirect object; *ring* is the direct object)

Exercise 64: The Indirect Object—Part I

Select the *direct* and *indirect object* in each of the sentences below, using the following form:

Indirect Object   *Direct Object*

1. Give me liberty.
2. I asked the soldier a question.
3. I will bring you the book Monday.
4. For many years he gave Mary flowers on her birthday.
5. Father gave me a pen and pencil.
6. Mike sent Fred and James some books and a magazine.
7. The cowboy taught his horse many useful tricks.
8. Show them the way to the beach.
9. The guard asked my father and me many questions.
10. Leonard sold Jerry two little rabbits.
11. Ben offered me an apple.
12. The postman handed me several letters.
13. We sent the children some candy and fruit for Christmas.
14. Will you lend me your book?
15. Show the pupils their marks.
16. You surely owe me an apology.
17. Sing us a song, Miss Jones.
18. Did you write your mother a letter?
19. Mother bought Fred, James and Henry books, toys

and games on their birthdays.
20. You should not have told him that story.

Exercise 65: The Indirect Object—Part II

Select the *direct* and *indirect object* in each of the sentences below, using the following form:

Indirect Object   *Direct Object*

1. That incident surely taught me a good lesson.
2. Mother will read us some interesting poetry.
3. Mr. Otis will read the class an interesting story.
4. Mr. Franks offered me a good position.
5. I will hand the postman these letters.
6. You owe me a dime, Ruth.

7. Martin threw Fred the ball.

8. The teacher gave us new books.
9. The spectators gave the players three rousing cheers.
10. He might get us some.
11. Louise sent me several letters last summer.

12. John's father bought him a pony and a saddle for his birthday.
13. I send Mary and her brother a box of fruit every month.
14. The guide will show you Fort Marion.
15. We gave them free tickets to the rodeo.
16. We bought our little dog a bone.
17. Give Bob and Henry a box of candy.
18. I gave my mother a ring on her anniversary.
19. The principal gave the graduating class some last-minute instructions.

20. Cut me a large piece of pie, please.

26. The Objective Complement

An **objective complement** is a second object coming after a direct object. The objective complement describes or explains the direct object and completes the meaning of the verb.

> The team elected Joe its *captain*.

An adjective also may be used as the objective complement.

> The rain made the trail *muddy*.

Exercise 66: The Objective Complement

Select the *direct object* and the *objective complement,* using the following form:

Direct Object	*Objective Complement*

1. The umpire declared our team the victor.
2. Father painted our camp white and red.
3. I will appoint you monitor.
4. I never did find him reliable.
5. I appointed him chairman of the group.

6. They named the child Mildred.
7. Did the boys choose Charlie captain of the basketball team?
8. Did you sweep the rug clean?
9. Mr. Larson may make you his partner.
10. She colored the eggs blue and red.
11. They later proved the statement false.
12. Do you always find him ready?
13. Why don't you nominate Margaret and Helen delegates to the convention?

14. Work usually makes us strong.

15. Fear struck him dumb.
16. We named our camp "Idlewood."
17. Leave the doors and windows open.
18. Do you think they will hold him responsible?
19. We named our new dog Lassie.
20. The class elected Howard president.

27. Predicate Words

Predicate words are words used after certain verbs known as copulative or linking verbs to describe or refer to the subject of the sentence.

The following are the most common copulative verbs: be (is, are, am, was, were), become, sound, taste, smell, seem, feel, look, grow, appear, resemble, etc.

There are three classes of predicate words:

1. The **predicate noun** is a noun which follows a copulative verb and denotes the same person or thing as the subject.

   Bob is my *friend*.   Tom became a *sailor*.

2. The **predicate pronoun** is a pronoun which follows a copulative verb and denotes or stands for the same person or thing as the subject.

   John was *he*.   It's *she,* all right.

3. The **predicate adjective** is an adjective which follows a copulative verb and describes the subject.

   The sky looks *blue*.   The cake tastes *good*.

Exercise 67: Predicate Words—Part I

Select the *predicate words* in the following **sentences:**

1. Texas is the largest state in the Union.
2. Jim looked tired after the race.
3. It was he who called.
4. My uncle was the man who built this house.
5. The rose smells sweet.
6. This is a very interesting book.
7. Mary's work seems perfect.
8. It was I at the door.
9. The boys looked tired and hungry.
10. These flowers resemble roses.
11. John appeared calm and brave.
12. Jim is my best friend.
13. These flowers smell very fragrant.
14. If you were I, would you accept his invitation?
15. After a while, she became bored with the story.
16. It was she who called.
17. Dad is a good tennis player.
18. The water feels too cold for swimming today.
19. To all of us the picture seemed unreal.
20. Thomas Jefferson was the founder of the University of Virginia.

Exercise 68: Predicate Words—Part II

Select the *predicate words* in the following sentences:

1. Harold is the youngest boy in the class.
2. All evening Mother seemed terribly worried.
3. Key West is the southernmost city in the United States.
4. The candy tastes too sweet.
5. He seems very nice.
6. The surf sounds booming.
7. He became a famous lawyer.
8. Mary is a dependable girl.
9. He is Bob Crane, our neighbor.
10. I noticed you were inattentive during the recitation.
11. Do you believe he will ever become more serious?
12. There is Mr. Hobbs, the principal of our school.
13. If you were she, would you have waited?
14. My little brother felt happy and contented.
15. The sky looked gray and dull.
16. That is she now at the door.
17. It was a beautiful warm June day.
18. Spring is the nicest season of the year.
19. This exercise seems very easy.
20. She appears taller every day.

28. *Independent Elements*

An **independent element** is a word or phrase or clause that has no grammatical connection with the sentence in which it is found. These independent elements (sometimes called **parenthetical elements**) are separated from the rest of the sentence by some mark of punctuation.

A. Words used independently—

1. Interjections:

> *Oh!* Here it is now.

2. Nominative of address:

> *Rose,* here are your books.

3. Transitional words (words such as *therefore, however, furthermore, besides, well, then*) used parenthetically within the sentence or at the beginning of the sentence. These words show the connection of the sentence in which you find them with some sentence which has come before.

> This, *however,* is not what I asked for.

> *Besides,* I can't walk that far.

B. Phrases used independently—

Phrases used parenthetically in a sentence and having no grammatical connection with the sentence are used independently. They show shifts in meaning, or introduce contrasts in ideas, or indicate the attitude of the speaker toward what is being said.

In any case, you are not at fault.

The grades in this school, *generally speaking,* are good.

After all, it wasn't your fault.

C. Clauses used independently—

Some clauses when introduced parenthetically within a sentence, and having no grammatical connection with the sentence, are used independently. They serve as side remarks by the speaker.

You will, *I suppose,* do as you want to.

You are entirely right, *I must admit.*

Exercise 69: Independent Elements

Select the *independent elements* in each of the following sentences:

1. Listen! What was that?
2. Yes, Fred, we will come.

3. You will, of course, go to the shore next summer.
4. Bob will, I fear, fail this course unless he works harder.
5. Well, of all things! Where did this come from?
6. By the way, what did you do with my pen?
7. Will we see you, then, at the dance?
8. This is my best hat, believe it or not.
9. Mother exclaimed, "Dear me, I told you about it this morning."
10. As you were saying, it doesn't really matter.
11. Well, Jane, why don't you answer?
12. "Well done, John," said Mrs. Lewis.
13. You have, I agree, a good alibi.
14. Oh, by the way, George, where is your last assignment?
15. Pshaw! I know you mean it, my good friend.
16. It was, indeed, a surprise to me.
17. Ruth, will you have lunch with me?
18. I will, nevertheless, ask him about it.
19. You are right, Tony, I must admit.
20. Let me explain, Rose.

29. The Appositive

An **appositive** is a noun element placed after another noun or pronoun to describe or explain it. The noun element in apposition and all its modifiers must be separated from the rest of the sentence by commas.

An **appositive word:**

My friend, *John,* is very loyal.

An **appositive phrase:**

Bob Jones, *the president of our class,* is a star football player.

An **appositive clause:**

That fact, *that prices have risen,* should make us more economical.

Exercise 70: The Appositive

Select the *appositive* in each of the following sentences.

1. Boston, the capital of Massachusetts, is a very large city.

2. The hope, that he would soon be here, kept us very happy.

3. I read several poems by Lowell, the popular American poet.

4. Mother lives in Los Angeles, the largest city in California.

5. Alaska, which will be my home, is the land of opportunity.

6. Have you ever read a book by Henry James, the novelist?

7. The fear, that they might lose the championship, made the boys fight hard.

8. My wish, that she would come to the party, was gratified.

9. The first boy, James by name, is at fault.

10. Do you remember Will Rogers, the world-famous humorist?

11. A large tree, a stately palm, is just outside our sunporch.

12. They spent the winter in Switzerland, the playground of Europe.

13. Our old car, a Pierce Arrow, is only fit for the Smithsonian Museum.

14. She lives in the next city, Rochester.
15. The order, that everyone appear in the auditorium, aroused great curiosity.
16. We talked to Mrs. Jones, the owner of the dog.
17. The thought, that I might win the contest, kept me interested for months.
18. Henry Taylor, although injured, ran a good race.
19. California, the land of sunshine and flowers, has always been my home.

20. Have you met Tom Jones, the captain of our team?

30. The Nominative of Address

The **nominative of address** is a noun or pronoun used independently in speaking directly to some person, place or thing. The nominative of address is separated from the rest of the sentence by a comma or by commas. We often find nominatives of address in imperative sentences where the subject *(you)* is understood.

Mary, (you) come here now.

Here, *Dad,* are your slippers.

Well, *folks,* (you) step right up.

Exercise 71: The Nominative of Address

Select the *nominative of address* in each of the following sentences:

1. Bob, close the door.
2. Why, Jerry, are you always late?
3. Noble oak, shelter me from the storm.
4. Mother said, "Ruth, you must be more ambitious."
5. Do you know, Martin, why I called for you?
6. Rome, thou hast been a mother to me.
7. Barbara and Mary, you may leave now.

8. Listen, girls, to what I have to say.

9. Here, Rover, come here.
10. Yes, Irene, you may go now.
11. Rover, lie down.
12. Mrs. Miles, may I speak to you?
13. Ladies and gentlemen, give me your attention.
14. James, don't go now.
15. But, my dear friend, you must do it now.
16. Now, class, please give me your attention.
17. Boys, please be quiet.
18. Here, Louis, is your hat.
19. My, Sam, how tired you look!
20. Friends and neighbors, I welcome you.

31. *The Expletives*

An **expletive** is a word used to introduce the real subject which follows the predicate.

There are two expletives, *it* and *there*.

It is easy *to swim* in salt water.
    (*it* is an expletive, *to swim* the subject)

There are ten *dimes* on the table.
    (*there* is an expletive, *dimes* the subject)

Exercise 72: The Expletives

Select the *expletive* and the *subject* in each of the sentences below, using the following form:

    Expletives   *Subjects*

1. It is hard to carry these heavy bundles.
2. I am sure it won't do any good to complain about it.
3. There goes Uncle Richard in his new car.
4. It was his idea to return early.
5. There's my father crossing the street.
6. It may be advisable to call Aunt Molly first.

7. It is easy to see his point of view.
8. There are thirty days in this month.
9. It was a mistake to blame Joe for our loss.

10. There were many people at the concert.

32. Tense of Verbs

Tense means time. Tense of verbs refers to the time of the action or condition.

The **present tense** is that form of the verb which indicates present time.

I *laugh.*   I *see.*

The **past tense** is that form of the verb which indicates past time.

I *laughed.*   I *saw.*

The **future tense** is that form of the verb which indicates future time.

I *shall laugh.*   I *will see.*

The **present perfect tense** is that form of the verb which indicates that the action is complete (or perfect) at the present time. The present perfect tense is formed by using *has* or *have* with the past participle of the verb.

He *has walked* for two hours already.

They *have seen* him every day.

The **past perfect tense** is that form of the verb which indicates that the action was complete (or perfect) at some time in the past. It is formed by using *had* with the past participle of the verb.

They *had finished* before I arrived.

The **future perfect tense** is that form of the verb which indicates that the action of the verb will be complete (or perfect) at some time in the future. It is formed by using *shall have* or *will have* with the past participle of the verb.

Before you come home, I *shall have left*.

Exercise 73: Tense of Verbs—Part I

Give the *tense* of the verb in the principal clause, using the following form:

      Verb   *Tense*

1. He left at noon.
2. Where have you been all day?
3. They will have begun it before you arrive.
4. All the work now lies before us.
5. Shall you be here next week?
6. I am ready now.
7. They will have eaten it all long before you arrive.
8. They bade him goodbye.

9. They had already bidden him goodbye when we arrived.
10. This picture has hung here for years.
11. We shall have driven five hundred miles by dusk tonight.
12. Cold winds sweep down from the North.
13. They had knelt there for hours.
14. I saw them yesterday.
15. She has known Joseph for five years.
16. Raise the bar higher.
17. Drink all of it.
18. Miss Bibbs has taught for forty years.
19. The puppy hid the bone under the chair.
20. They have always drunk from this stream.

Exercise 74: Tense of Verbs—Part II

Give the *tense* of the verb in the principal clause, using the following form:

Verb   *Tense*

1. Some people are very lazy.
2. Mary has not swept the floor.
3. I am he.
4. Shall I beat the rug?
5. John had become a successful business man.
6. Read it aloud.
7. She shall have proved it then, I am sure.

8. He went to town on **his** pony.

9. You will have then taught our whole family.
10. You certainly had an interesting report.
11. Have they raised the old boat yet?
12. He went in a great hurry.
13. Have they forgiven us yet?
14. Give it to me, Randy.
15. They bore their burdens well.
16. Then I shall have proved it to you.
17. The birds have flown South again.
18. All the water had flowed out of the bucket.
19. Mother has thrown them all away.

20. He will show me the way.

Exercise 75: Tense of Verbs—Part III

Illustrate each of the following in a sentence of your own:

1. past of *fly*
2. present perfect of *write*
3. present perfect of *shine*
4. past of *weep*
5. future perfect of *hide*
6. past of *drink*
7. future of *shrink*
8. past perfect of *say*
9. present of *wear*
10. past of *set*
11. present perfect of *sit*
12. present of *choose*
13. past perfect of *speak*
14. past of *choose*
15. past perfect of *do*
16. present perfect of *do*
17. future perfect of *teach*
18. future of *drive*
19. past of *live*
20. past perfect of *go*

33. Main and Auxiliary Verbs

A **verb phrase** consists of the main (or principal) verb with its auxiliary (or helper) verb or verbs.

You *should have seen* her play tennis.

> Verb phrase: *should have seen*
> Main verb: *seen*
> Auxiliary verbs: *should have*

Auxiliary verbs help the main verb by expressing the exact shade of meaning. The auxiliary verbs are: be, is, are, am, was, were, has, have, had, has been, had been, do, does, did, done, may, might, can, could, shall, should, will, would, must.

Auxiliary verbs are used to form interrogative sentences.

Should I not *have gone* home?

Did you *call* me?

In a compound predicate, the same auxiliary verb is understood to form the second main verb.

You *will visit* us and (*will*) *stay* overnight.

Exercise 76: Main and Auxiliary Verbs—Part I

Select the *main* and *auxiliary verbs,* using the following form:

Auxiliary Verbs   *Main Verbs*

1. Mother hurriedly had called the store.
2. They could not be clearly heard from the balcony.
3. Did he too get tired?
4. I can not arrive home until Sunday.
5. I will not return it.
6. I am not planning to go.
7. Many people have been patiently waiting for some news of the ship.
8. What picture did you see at the movies yesterday?
9. My dog can now easily do that trick.
10. The accident must have been seen by several people.
11. The tower was brilliantly lighted every night.
12. He does not try very hard.

13. The troop of scouts must have traveled onward.

14. The description of the lost man has already been broadcasted over the radio.
15. Will you not be too tired?
16. You must have met John yesterday.
17. He did not see me at all.
18. Down the road were two boys chasing the little dog.
19. When did you arrive?
20. Is our semester ending earlier this year?

Exercise 77: Main and Auxiliary Verbs—Part II

Select the *main* and *auxiliary verbs,* using the following form:

    Auxiliary Verbs   *Main Verbs*

1. Couldn't he see you?
2. I will not leave early.
3. Does your father help you?
4. Why don't you leave later?
5. I could have seen the man and called to him.
6. They were rarely seen at the movies.
7. They could hardly read the letter.
8. Bob hesitatingly had put the rifle in its place.
9. The dog will sit up and beg for his food.
10. Don't look now!
11. Doesn't that noise annoy you?

12. Betty has gone for a walk with her grandfather.

13. Did you ever see such a sight?
14. By noon I shall have finished all my work.
15. Do bring me some ice-cream at once.
16. These lines must be very clearly traced.
17. They do not seem pleased.
18. If you do not work hard, you certainly can not expect to pass.
19. They don't especially like Mary, but they will not ignore her.
20. Jerry can sell newspapers and mow lawns during his vacation.

34. Principal Parts of Verbs

Every verb has three forms which are so important that they are called the **principal parts.** These principal parts are (1) the present tense, (2) the past tense, and (3) the past participle.

Verbs which form the past tense and past participle by adding *d* or *ed* to the present tense are called **regular verbs.**

> *Present tense:* laugh
> *Past tense:* laughed
> *Past participle:* laughed

Verbs which form the past tense and past participle irregularly by a change in spelling, etc., are called **irregular verbs.**

> *Present tense:* drink
> *Past tense:* drank
> *Past participle:* drunk

Principal Parts of Some Troublesome Verbs

Present Tense	*Past Tense*	*Past Participle*
am (be)	was	been
arise	arose	arisen
attack	attacked	attacked
awake	awoke	awaked
bear	bore	borne, or born
beat	beat	beaten
become	became	become
begin	began	begun
bend	bent	bent
bite	bit	bitten
bleed	bled	bled
blow	blew	blown
break	broke	broken
bring	brought	brought
burn	burned, or burnt	burned, or burnt
burst	burst	burst
catch	caught	caught
choose	chose	chosen
climb	climbed	climbed
come	came	come
creep	crept	crept
dig	dug	dug
dive	dived	dived
do	did	done

Present Tense	Past Tense	Past Participle
drag	dragged	dragged
draw	drew	drawn
dream	dreamed, or dreamt	dreamed, or dreamt
drink	drank	drunk
drive	drove	driven
drown	drowned	drowned
dwell	dwelt, or dwelled	dwelt
eat	ate	eaten
fall	fell	fallen
fight	fought	fought
flee	fled	fled
flow	flowed	flowed
fly	flew	flown
forget	forgot	forgotten
forgive	forgave	forgiven
freeze	froze	frozen
get	got	got
give	gave	given
go	went	gone
grow	grew	grown
hang (to suspend)	hung	hung
hang (to execute)	hanged	hanged

Present Tense	*Past Tense*	*Past Participle*
hear	heard	heard
heat	heated	heated
hide	hid	hidden
hold	held	held
hurt	hurt	hurt
kneel	knelt	knelt
know	knew	known
lay (to put)	laid	laid
lead	led	led
lend	lent	lent
lie (to recline)	lay	lain
lie (to tell a lie)	lied	lied
light	lighted, or lit	lighted, or li
lose	lost	lost
mean	meant	meant
mistake	mistook	mistaken
pay	paid	paid
plead	pleaded	pleaded
prove	proved	proved, or proven
read	read	read
rid	rid	rid
ride	rode	ridden
ring	rang	rung
rise	rose	risen

Present Tense	Past Tense	Past Participle
run	ran	run
say	said	said
see	saw	seen
set	set	set
sew	sewed	sewed, or sewn
shake	shook	shaken
shine	shone	shone
show	showed	showed, or shown
shrink	shrank	shrunk
sing	sang	sung
sink	sank	sunk
sit	sat	sat
slay	slew	slain
slide	slid	slid
speak	spoke	spoken
spend	spent	spent
spit	spit, or spat	spit, or spat
spring	sprang	sprung
steal	stole	stolen
strike	struck	struck
swear	swore	sworn
sweep	swept	swept
swim	swam	swum
take	took	taken
teach	taught	taught
tear	tore	torn

Present Tense	Past Tense	Past Participle
throw	threw	thrown
thrust	thrust	thrust
undertake	undertook	undertaken
wake	woke, or waked	waked, or wakened
wear	wore	worn
weave	wove	woven
weep	wept	wept
wind	wound	wound
wring	wrung	wrung
write	wrote	written

Exercise 78: Principal Parts of Verbs—Part I

Select the form of the verb in parenthesis that correctly completes the tense of the sentence:

1. The ship (sank, sunk) very rapidly.

2. My dog has never (bit, bitten) anyone.

3. He (drank, drunk) the fruit juice.
4. I (hanged, hung) the coat on the hanger.
5. I (seen, saw) the car speeding down the road.

6. I (give, gave) him the money yesterday.
7. They have (hanged, hung) several of the men.
8. It was (tore, torn) when I received it.
9. He has (become, became) a skilled worker.
10. The men had (rode, ridden) over the same road for years.
11. I am sure he (did, done) the best he could.
12. I nearly (freezed, froze) while waiting for you.
13. The fruit has (fell, fallen) into the water.
14. It is good that the wound has (bled, bleed) freely
15. The sun has (shone, shown) for thirty days.
16. The boys (sung, sang) all the old songs.
17. I (saw, seen) it myself.
18. Mary has (drank, drunk) two glasses of water.
19. The dish is (broke, broken).
20. My father (teached, taught) me to drive.

Exercise 79: Principal Parts of Verbs—Part II

Select the form of the verb in parenthesis that correctly completes the tense of the sentence:

1. Was your picture (took, taken)?
2. Helen (brung, brought) me the letter.
3. Who (rung, rang) the bell?
4. The boy had (stole, stolen) the apples.
5. John (wrote, written) the lesson rapidly.
6. Last Tuesday Paul (gave, give) me a gift.

7. It was (stole, stolen) last night.
8. Has he (ate, eaten) all his lunch?
9. Richard and Jerry have (gone, went) to the football game.
10. Mother (seen, saw) many interesting things.
11. The dog (sprang, sprung) up when he saw his master.
12. He should have (took, taken) no chances.
13. The teacher said he (saw, seen) the dog last night.
14. I was amazed to see how much the child had (growed, grown).
15. The boy could not have (sang, sung) more than three songs.
16. They would not have been (beat, beaten) if George had been playing.
17. I don't think she could have (bore, borne) much more.
18. Aunt Ann has (gone, went) to the post office.
19. Has the lake (frozen, froze) enough for skating?
20. He said he had (swam, swum) the river before.

Exercise 80: Principal Parts of Verbs—Part III

Select the form of the verb in parenthesis that correctly completes the tense of the sentence:

1. He (throwed, threw) the ball into the river.
2. Who (drank, drunk) my tea?
3. Who (teared, tore) the picture?

4. The boys (choosed, chose) Fred to be their captain.

5. Tom said that he did not (chose, choose) to run again for the captaincy.

6. The dog would not have (bit, bitten) you if you had been careful.

7. We (drank, drunk) two quarts of milk today.

8. If I had (knew, known) it, I would not have let him go.

9. The girls (swam, swum) in the cold water.

10. The sun had (shined, shone) all day.

11. We have (drove, driven) fifty miles already.

12. Martin has (eaten, ate) too much pie.

13. The salesman had (shone, shown) us several samples.

14. Have you (forgot, forgotten) your books?

15. Have you (heared, heard) the good news?

16. If you had worked harder, you would have (became, become) a manager.

17. The cat was almost (drownded, drowned).

18. Is the pen (broke, broken)?

19. Have you (rode, ridden) all day?

20. Have you (wrote, written) that letter yet?

Exercise 81: Principal Parts of Verbs—Part IV

Write the appropriate form of the verb in parenthesis:

1. Have you (wear) your new suit yet?

2. I (see) you yesterday.

3. Have you (write) to him yet?
4. They have (choose) all of them.
5. They had (throw) them all away.
6. I have (show) him all the snapshots.
7. The little child had (fall) from the pony.
8. How long have you (drive) a car?
9. I (ride) there last year.
10. Has he (forgive) you?
11. Has he (speak) to you about the picnic?
12. The plate (fall) from her hands.
13. I hope I have (do) my share.
14. I don't see why he (undertake) such a task.
15. She has (grow) at least an inch since Christmas
16. They all quickly (dive) into the water.
17. We have (go) there many times.
18. The cat (spring) upon the dog.

19. He (catch) the ball on the
   bound.

20. Mother (sew) all evening.

Exercise 82: Principal Parts of Verbs—Part V

Write the appropriate form of the verb in parenthesis:

1. Army had (beat) Navy by one touchdown.
2. She (sing) the song well last night.
3. They did (drink) as much milk as they could.
4. Has Ralph (go) to the movies yet?
5. We were almost (freeze) on our trip.
6. Have you (begin) the lesson yet?
7. If he had (swim) faster, he could have won the race.
8. My trousers (shrink) when they were washed.
9. He (throw) water on the fire.
10. The window was (break) last night.
11. Frank was (choose) leader of the squad.
12. I have (arise) early all summer.
13. She has (eat) two meals today.
14. The old man (come) for the package.
15. Mother has (shrink) my sweater so that I can't wear it.
16. Have you ever (ride) before?
17. Last year the wind (blow) our tent down.
18. The mail carrier (come) late yesterday.
19. I have never (swim) that far before.
20. You have (give) me a clue.

35. Some Troublesome Pairs of Verbs

Bring—Take

Bring means to carry something toward the speaker or place.

Take means to carry something away from the speaker or place to another person or place.

Exercise 83: Bring—Take

Use *bring* or *take* in each of the following sentences:

1. _____ this letter to the office.
2. Please _____ me that book on your desk.
3. Jerry, _____ this package home.
4. May I _____ this to the library?

5. Please _____ this note to the principal.

6. I shall _____ them to the car.
7. _____ me that book.
8. _____ this away.
9. Please _____ me a glass of water.
10. _____ me his answer immediately.

May—Can

Can means ability.

May means permission or possibility.

Exercise 84: May—Can

Use *may* or *can* in each of the following sentences:

1. _____ I take the job?
2. You know I _____ do the work.
3. _____ I go to the movies?
4. _____ Joe go with me?
5. John _____ spell as well as Tom.
6. Mother says we _____ go to the movies.
7. _____ I use the telephone?
8. You _____ take the car.
9. _____ I see the full report?
10. _____ you prove you are a licensed driver?

Lie—Lay

Lie (lay, lying, lain) means to rest, recline or occupy a position. It is always intransitive (it has *no* object).

Lay (laid, laying, laid) means to put or to place, or to cause a person or a thing to lie. It is always transitive (it has an object).

Exercise 85: Lie—Lay—Part I

Use the proper form of *lie* or *lay* in each of the following sentences:

1. Where did you _____ the book?
2. I _____ down and slept for two hours.
3. My dog _____ before the fireplace and slept.
4. Your book has been _____ there all day.
5. Who _____ it there?
6. Did the book _____ on the porch all night?
7. Mother _____ down for a nap each afternoon this week.
8. It seemed as though the whole summer _____ before us.
9. The cat had been _____ in the chair.
10. I am _____ on the ground.
11. The old ship had _____ on the harbor bottom for many years.
12. I had _____ awake all night.
13. I shall _____ down until you come.

14. The cat is _____ on a rug before the fire.
15. The company has _____ down a new pavement on the street.
16. I had _____ there since you left.
17. The woman _____ there and never stirred.
18. Don't _____ your coat on that chair.
19. Under a tree the little bear was _____.
20. The beautiful country _____ before us.

Exercise 86: Lie—Lay—Part II

Use the proper form of *lie* or *lay* in each of the following sentences:

1. When will the concrete be _____?
2. "_____ down and rest," said the doctor.

3. The pirates were surprised to see what _____ in the hold of the ship.

4. _____ the silverware in the chest.
5. She _____ down each day at three and has a cup of tea.

6. The sidewalk was _____ in a week.
7. The teacher _____ down the book and looked at me.
8. The men _____ away their tools and sat down.
9. _____ down and rest for ten minutes.
10. She has _____ there all morning.
11. Mother _____ her sewing away.
12. Where did you _____ my papers?
13. She _____ down and rested all day.
14. The dog _____ before the open door and **yawns.**
15. Your pen has _____ there all night.
16. Many articles were found _____ on the ground.
17. I _____ the money on the counter.
18. Mother _____ awake and made plans.
19. We were amazed to see what he _____ before us on the table.
20. The officer _____ his hand on the weeping child's shoulder.

Sit—Set

Sit (sat, sitting, sat) means to rest or perch; to assume a sitting position. It is always intransitive (it has *no* object).

Set (set, setting, set) means to put or place something; to place something in position. It is usually transitive (it usually has an object).

Exercise 87: Sit—Set—Part I

Use the proper form of *sit* or *set* in each of the following sentences:

1. The teacher _____ the time when we should return.
2. When we returned home, we found the dog _____ there just as we had left her.
3. She always _____ there and waits for us.
4. In the North they often _____ traps in the winter
5. Shall we _____ here for a while?
6. All day yesterday she _____ on the porch of her cottage.
7. The fishermen _____ their nets.
8. Did you _____ your watch correctly?
9. Mr. and Mrs. Brown have always _____ in the front row.
10. The children _____ up the ping pong table.
11. I shall _____ at the speaker's table.
12. We had _____ the candy on the shelf to cool.
13. _____ the chairs on the lawn.
14. The maid _____ the pitcher of lemonade on the table.
15. We often just _____ and looked at the beautiful flowers.
16. Do you intend to _____ there all day?
17. The girls did not _____ the table very attractively.

18. She would often _____ up all night reading.
19. We have been _____ here for hours.
20. The girls _____ in the sun all day today.

Exercise 88: Sit—Set—Part II

Use the proper form of *sit* or *set* in each of the following sentences:

1. Please _____ the salad in the refrigerator.
2. Shall we _____ the books on the table?
3. They have always _____ in the front row.
4. We _____ the table before we went to bed.
5. He was _____ up pins at the bowling alley.
6. Father is _____ in the shade.
7. _____ the fruit in the refrigerator.
8. Dad has always _____ at the head of the table.
9. The pupils were _____ in their seat when I arrived.
10. I always _____ my clock with the radio.
11. I _____ in this seat last year.
12. Is she still _____ the table?
13. _____ Mother's knitting on the porch.
14. We _____ the pail of water on the floor.
15. She _____ there for an hour, lost in thought.
16. We just _____ for more than an hour looking at the scenery.

17. They _____ nets to catch some small fish.
18. I like to _____ and dream.
19. She _____ there for hours and didn't say a word.
20. After we had _____ the table, we _____ down to rest.

Rise—Raise

Rise (rose, rising, risen) means to reach a higher point; to go up. It is always intransitive (it does *not* have an object).

Raise (raised, raising, raised) means to lift up; to reach a higher point. It is always transitive (it always has an object).

Exercise 89: Rise—Raise—Part I

Use the proper form of *rise* or *raise* in each of the following sentences:

1. As one person, the crowd _____ from their seats.
2. His job each morning is to _____ the flag.
3. I expected him to _____ early.
4. Baking powder causes cakes to _____.
5. I wanted to see if the sun had _____.
6. The teacher _____ his voice above the noise.
7. Our class in English has been _____ money for a poor family.
8. Joe _____ and sang a song.

9. I had just _____ the window when the storm broke.

10. The forest ranger had _____ early.

11. The men _____ the ladder and began to work.

12. The _____ river caused great alarm.

13. Having at last _____ to her feet, she was too frightened to speak.

14. Mother had just _____ the window when the blast came.

15. _____ the curtain and see who is at the door.

16. I thought that I was _____ very early, but everyone else was already up.

17. When at camp last summer, we always _____ very early for a swim before breakfast.

18. At last the principal _____ to speak to us.

19. The temperature _____ twenty degrees before noon.

20. The sun had hardly _____ when we were up.

Exercise 90: Rise—Raise—Part II

Use the proper form of *rise* or *raise* in each of the following sentences:

1. Tom _____ and spoke.
2. Will you _____ the bucket for me?
3. If you _____ early, you will enjoy it.
4. Don has _____ the window.
5. He _____ the flag and started the race.
6. The crowd _____ to its feet and cheered.
7. The cake _____ high on one side.
8. Will you please _____ the window for me?
9. He is accustomed to _____ early.
10. On the farm we _____ with the birds.
11. Will you _____ the box for me?
12. If you _____ early, you may go too.
13. She had just _____ the curtain when the lightning struck the tree.
14. The cake had _____ too high in the center.
15. He carefully _____ the cover of the old box.
16. Look and see if the moon has _____.
17. The old man politely _____ his hat to the ladies.
18. The bread was _____ only in the middle.
19. I was so surprised when Tommy _____ and spoke.
20. He was _____ the lid and peeking in.

Exercise 91: Lie—Lay, Sit—Set, Rise—Raise— Part I

Use the proper form of *lie, lay, sit, set, rise, raise* in the following sentences:

1. The teacher s_____ the hour of our appointment.
2. After much thought, he r_____ and made his plea.
3. They all s_____ on the bench.
4. The boys watched her r_____ the cover of the box and s_____ the trap.
5. The balloon had r_____ only a few feet when it exploded.
6. L_____ on your back for ten weeks is surely not my idea of a vacation.
7. The dog l_____ on the lawn and wants to be petted.
8. After I had r_____ to speak, I found that I had entirely forgotten my speech.
9. Please r_____ the window and s_____ the pies on the ledge.
10. After the sun had r_____, we l_____ down under a large tree.
11. The glider r_____ quickly and vanished among the clouds.
12. L_____ the boxes on the floor and s_____ in this chair for a few minutes.

13. The course of the ship had been s_____ by the captain.

14. We r_____ funds for the Red Cross.

15. The man r_____ the fallen wreath and put it into position.

16. The trout were l_____ in pools of water.

17. We s_____ the table for breakfast before the others had r_____.

18. She opened the door and s_____ the bottle on the steps.

19. The plans were carefully l_____.

20. Mother had r_____ early to get the children ready.

Exercise 92: Lie—Lay, Sit—Set, Rise—Raise— Part II

Use the proper form of *lie, lay, sit, set, rise, raise* in the following sentences:

1. Finally he r_____ from his chair and r_____ his hand.

2. Where did you s_____ the candy?

3. I s_____ down after a while.

4. We had just r_____ the awning when the storm broke.

5. The U.N. has l_____ down the rules for international relations.

6. She has l_____ there for hours.

7. This is the table which she has s_____ for her party.

8. Last night as she r_____ to sing, the audience r_____ their voices in loud approval.

9. S_____ the chairs on the back lawn.

10. He had just l_____ down when I called.

11. Before the sun had r_____, we were on our way to camp.

12. You must s_____ still during the test.

13. L_____ down your pencil!

14. When the mist had r_____, we found that we were lost.

15. You should always r_____ the window before you l_____ down.

16. You may l_____ away your work now.

17. We s_____ some traps.

18. They s_____ the captain on their shoulders and marched around the field.

19. Before I l_____ down, I shall finish this letter.

20. Helen s_____ the table before the sun had r_____.

Exercise 93: Lie—Lay, Sit—Set, Rise—Raise—Part III

Use the proper form of *lie, lay, sit, set, rise, raise* in the following sentences:

1. When my father sleeps, he always l_____ with his arms above his head.

2. At our house last summer, everyone r_____ very early and s_____ out for work in the factory.

3. I don't see how he could have r_____ that huge rock alone.

4. He always r_____ his hat when he meets a lady.

5. We r_____ the flag in silent tribute every morning.

6. The children s_____ on the sidelines and cheered.

7. After the fog had r_____, we were surprised to see where our ship was l_____.

8. She always s_____ there and waits for me.

9. When I r_____ the window, I was amazed at what I saw.

10. The balloon had r_____ to an unbelievable height.

11. Then, a moment later, they r_____ from their seats as one man.

12. They will l_____ the whole thing before the Student Council.

13. Quickly he r_____ the curtain.
14. Mother s_____ the table before she left.
15. She has always l_____ the books where they would not get wet.
16. Thousands of men have been working for months, l_____ the huge pipeline.
17. The men s_____ their nets last night.
18. The little boy l_____ his toys in my lap and screams in delight.
19. The children s_____ in the sun all afternoon.
20. The doctor said, "L_____ down and get some sleep."

Shall—Will

To express simple future time on the part of the speaker:

Use *shall* if the subject is in the first person.

Use *will* if the subject is in the second or third person.

I *shall* leave soon.	We *shall* leave soon.
You *will* leave soon.	You *will* leave soon.
He *will* leave soon.	They *will* leave soon.

To express promise, determination, resolution, desire or willingness on the part of the speaker:

Use *will* if the subject is in the first person.

Use *shall* if the subject is in the second or third person.

I *will* go.   We *will* go.

You *shall* go.   You *shall* go.

He *shall* go.   They *shall* go.

In questions, the verb used depends upon the answer expected. Use in the question the verb needed in the answer: "*Will* you vote for me?" (Answer expected: "I *will*.")

Exercise 94: Shall—Will—Part I

Use *shall* or *will* in each of the following sentences:

1. We _____ be glad to have you come to see us.
2. _____ you be here all winter?
3. I _____ go whether they do or not.
4. I _____ read every night for a week.
5. You _____ finish this paper before you leave the house.
6. John said he _____ wait for you.
7. If I have my way, the puppy _____ always have a good home.
8. We _____ be delighted to attend.
9. "I _____ help you if I am able," he promised.
10. "I _____ spend the summer at home," Bob said.

11. _____ she be able to keep this good position?
12. "You _____ do it when I say so," he shouted.
13. They _____ pay dearly for this!
14. He _____ be graduated in June.
15. I _____ be graduated in January.
16. _____ he really resign now?
17. When _____ you begin your new work?
18. Your friends _____ enjoy the party.
19. _____ you oblige us by singing at the party to-night?
20. I _____ lend him my tennis racket.

Exercise 95: Shall—Will—Part II

Use *shall* or *will* in each of the following sentences:

1. I promised Dad that I _____ never do that again.
2. _____ you promise not to tell anyone?
3. _____ the game be postponed?
4. If you _____ tell me, I _____ tell no one.
5. If you _____ lend me a dollar, I _____ repay you.
6. I _____ be glad to lend it to you.
7. I think I _____ go to the game.
8. _____ you be late to school if you do this errand for me?
9. You _____ find John at home.

10. Louise _____ return Monday.
11. We _____ be glad to call if it is at all possible.
12. Your sons _____ enjoy the vacation.
13. By this time Thursday I _____ be at home.
14. When _____ you begin your course?
15. How much _____ we spend on our Christmas gifts?
16. He _____. do as his father says.
17. I am sure you _____ enjoy your vacation at our camp
18. What _____ we take on our canoe trip?
19. You _____ do as the captain of the team tells you.
20. _____ you please call for me Saturday?

36. Transitive and Intransitive Verbs

A **transitive verb** requires a direct object to complete its meaning. Transitive means "passing or going over"; thus, the action of the verb goes from the subject over to the direct object.

She *combed* her hair.　　　He *painted* the barn.

An **intransitive verb** does not require a direct object to complete its meaning.

We *walked* around the park.　The ice *melted*.

Exercise 96: Transitive and Intransitive Verbs --Part I

Classify the verbs in the following sentences as *transitive* or *intransitive*. Show the direct object of the transitive verbs. Use the following form:

Intransitive　　*Transitive*　　*Direct Object*

1. We drove to the beach last Tuesday.
2. The water made holes in our tent.
3. Mother is preparing dinner.
4. Do you feel better now?

5. It has not rained for days.
6. The skaters skimmed across the pond.
7. Do you listen to the radio often?
8. The teacher read us a very interesting story.
9. Last night we went to the movies.
10. Will you go to the dance with me this evening?
11. Put the books on the desk in the library.
12. In our excitement we forgot our umbrella.
13. Where did you find these pencils?
14. Do you like poetry?
15. We sailed our boat in the lake.
16. We shall drive to Philadelphia for a day or two.
17. We planted several trees in our back yard.
18. These shrubs will grow quickly.
19. I like orange juice for breakfast.
20. Did you call Dad?

Exercise 97: Transitive and Intransitive Verbs —Part II

Classify the verbs in the following sentences as *transitive* or *intransitive*. Show the direct object of the transitive verbs. Use the following form:

Intransitive   *Transitive*   *Direct Object*

1. I had never read this poem before.
2. Do you like all kinds of citrus fruits?
3. Have you read the latest book of poems by Robert Frost?

4. Bob threw the ball into the basket.

5. You should not watch him so closely.
6. A radio wave travels around the world with the speed of sound.
7. The stature of a great man increases with the passing of time.
8. The boys won the cup easily.
9. You must stir it constantly.
10. Hunters and dogs followed the trail.
11. I went to the beach yesterday.
12. Do you like the summer?
13. We often watch the beautiful sunset.
14. She ate hastily and left.
15. Did your team win the cup this year?
16. The sun was shining brightly.
17. Last week our principal awarded the athletic and scholarship prizes.
18. What reason did she give for her absence?
19. We saw in the store windows some jewelry of great value.
20. Mother always does her share of everything.

37. Copulative Verbs

A **copulative** (or **linking**) **verb** is an intransitive verb which links its subject with a noun or pronoun (**predicate nominative**) meaning the same person or thing as the subject, or with an adjective (**predicate adjective**) modifying the subject.

> That boy *is Frank.*
>> (*Frank* is a predicate nominative after the copulative verb *is.*)

> She *became* a private *secretary.*
>> (*Secretary* is a predicate nominative after the copulative verb *became.*)

> Fresh coffee *smells good.*
>> (*Good* is a predicate adjective after the copulative verb *smells.*)

Some of the most common copulative verbs are: be (is, are, am, was, were), sound, taste, smell, feel, appear, keep, remain, stay, grow, seem, look, become, prove turn.

Caution: When one of these verbs has an object, it is used transitively; hence, it is not a copulative verb: He *tasted* the *coffee.*

Exercise 98: Copulative Verbs—Part I

Select the *copulative verbs* in the following sentences. Be careful of some verbs which are used transitively; that is, they have an object.

1. The soda tastes bitter.
2. The cookies were delicious.
3. Washington is the father of our country.
4. Marion is my cousin from New Orleans.
5. She tasted every cake.
6. You seem tired after your long ride.
7. The roses smell sweet.
8. Mr. Hanks became a famous politician.
9. That first problem was hard.
10. Fred turned the clock around.
11. Franklin Roosevelt became a great leader.
12. It was he on the telephone.
13. The boys have been pals for years.
14. John always appears cool.
15. The palms in the distance looked very beautiful.
16. The road seemed very rough to us.
17. In the North the leaves turn brown in the autumn
18. Yes, it was they.
19. You always seem tired.
20. The foreman sounded the whistle.

Exercise 99: Copulative Verbs—Part II

Select the *copulative verbs* in the following sentences. Be careful of some verbs which are used transitively; that is, they have an object.

1. The whistle sounded loud and clear.
2. My grandfather was a general.
3. Did the milk turn sour?
4. Most of our presidents have been college graduates.
5. Jack is my friend.
6. The tailor felt the quality of the cloth.
7. That boy is a regular clown.
8. Is English your favorite subject?
9. California is also a very desirable state in which to live.
10. John is the president of the graduating class.
11. After several years of study, she became a doctor.
12. I feel better today.
13. She kept the child in all day.
14. The night grew dark and windy.
15. It was he and she who called.
16. I tasted the syrup.
17. Does your house stay cool in the summer?
18. Mrs. Hicks is my aunt from Chicago.
19. The water feels too hot.
20. She is my only cousin.

38. Active and Passive Voice

Voice is a form of the verb which shows whether the subject performs the act or is acted upon.

A verb is in the **active voice** when the subject performs the act.

A verb is in the **passive voice** when the subject is acted upon.

Active voice: My father *built* the house.

Passive voice: The house *was built* by my father.

Note that the object in the active voice becomes the subject in the passive voice.

The passive voice always contains a helping verb.

The active voice usually expresses the idea of the sentence more effectively than the passive voice.

Exercise 100: Active and Passive Voice—Part 1

Select the verbs in the following sentences and tell whether each is in the *active* or *passive voice:*

1. Mother made some pies.
2. The teacher told an interesting story.
3. In the United States the president is elected by the people.

4. These cookies were baked by my sister.
5. Charles was punished by the teacher.
6. A long and exciting tale was told by the imaginative boy.
7. The audience was deeply touched by his thrilling experiences.
8. I ate two eggs for breakfast this morning.
9. A large black bear was shot by my brother.
10. Did you ever shoot a bear?
11. Marie paints very pretty pictures.
12. This one was painted by her in France.
13. The last speaker made a good impression.
14. Judge Brown gave them a good lecture.
15. The dog was struck by the little child.
16. Many songs were sung by the young tenor.
17. I saw a very exciting game.
18. Helen wrote two letters to Miriam last week.
19. A homer was made by the pinch hitter.

20. My brother wore an Oriental costume to the ball.

Exercise 101: Active and Passive Voice—Part II

Change each of the following sentences from the *passive* to the *active voice;* if it is already in the active voice, merely answer "Active."

1. The house was painted white by us.
2. Has a rainbow ever been seen by you?
3. A short story was written by Louise.
4. A little boy was bitten by the dog.
5. We were given some good advice by Uncle Ted.
6. They gave us two boxes of apples.
7. A new bicycle was given to her.
8. A prescription was written by the doctor.
9. Many games were played by the children.
10. Has Eddie been seen by you today?
11. He stood back of me.
12. A cheese sandwich was eaten by me for lunch.
13. An exciting book was read by me last night.
14. The American flag is loved by all of us.
15. Much destruction was caused by the high winds.
16. When did you finish your work?
17. She rode a horse along the path.
18. Has the pencil been sharpened by you?
19. A new suit was bought for me by Dad.
20. Did you see the circus?

39. Agreement of Verb with Subject

A verb should agree with its subject in person and number.

> There *was* a very tall *girl* in the office.
> (*girl* is the subject)

> There *were* two *pots* on the stove.
> (*pots* is the subject)

> A *box* of oranges *was* sent from Florida.
> (*box* is the subject)

> Two *girls,* besides Alice, *are* here.
> (*girls* is the subject)

Remember that *doesn't* is the contraction of *does not,* *don't* the contraction of *do not.*

> *Frank doesn't* swim well.

> Why *don't they* come?

Always use *were* with the subject *you.*

> *You were* (not *was*) late today.

A compound subject joined by *and* usually requires a plural verb.

John and *Mary are* at home.

If the parts of a compound subject are joined by *and* and mean the same person or thing, or represent a single idea or unit, a singular verb should be used.

The secretary and treasurer of our class *is* a boy.

Oatmeal and milk *constitutes* my father's breakfast.

If two or more singular subjects are joined by *or* or *nor,* use a singular verb.

Either Tom or Henry *is* at fault.

If two subjects are not in the same person or number, the verb should agree with the subject nearer to it.

Neither the girls nor *Fred is* at home.

Neither Fred nor the *girls are* at home.

The following indefinite pronouns are singular: *each, every, either, neither, one, everyone, any, anyone, nobody, each one, no one, someone, everybody, somebody, anybody.*

Someone was whistling loudly.

Every man, woman, and child *is* welcome.

A collective noun such as *team, club, audience, class,*

committee, army, band and *family* names a group. A collective noun is singular when it is thought of as a single unit, but plural when it is considered as a number of individuals.

Our team *is* sure to win today.
(*team* is considered as a single unit)

Our team *are* going to elect a captain today.
(*team* is considered as a number of individuals)

Nouns like the following are singular in meaning although plural in form: *civics, physics, news, measles, United States.*

Physics is a science.   The *news was* good.

Nouns like the following are always plural: *wages, trousers, clothes, scissors, thanks, riches, contents.*

His *wages were* paid.   Your *trousers are* long.

Nouns like the following may be singular or plural: *athletics, politics, means, pains, series, species.*

Exercise 102: Agreement of Verb with Subject —Part I

Select the verb in parenthesis that agrees in person and number with its subject:

1. There (was, were) a dog and a cat in the chair.

2. He (doesn't, don't) speak very well.
3. Each of the girls (observe, observes) all the restrictions.
4. Everybody (was, were) asked to remain seated.
5. It (doesn't, don't) seem possible.
6. The scissors (is, are) on the table.
7. Some members of the faculty (is, are) present.
8. There (is, are) a dog, a cat and a bird in the garage.
9. A magazine and a book (was, were) lying on the floor.
10. Civics (is, are) easy for Jane.
11. Interesting news (is, are) what sells our paper.
12. Neither of you (seem, seems) to be paying attention.
13. There (was, were) three hundred persons at the church.
14. My best friend and classmate (are, is) Jerry.
15. Either Frank or Mary (were, was) here.
16. The noise of the trucks (disturb, disturbs) my sister.
17. (Is, Are) each of the boys working now?
18. Neither of the boys (is, are) at home.
19. That kind of fruit (is, are) hard to get.
20. (Wasn't, Weren't) you here last year?

Exercise 103: Agreement of Verb with Subject —Part II

Select the verb in parenthesis that agrees in person and number with its subject:

1. There (go, goes) Bob and his dog.
2. How (is, are) your father and mother?
3. The Jones Furniture Company (is, are) having a special sale.
4. Only half of the material (was, were) there.
5. Only one of the boys (is, are) able to leave now
6. Why (doesn't, don't) he ask the way?
7. (Is, Are) everyone of the lessons done?
8. (Doesn't, Don't) either of you care for dessert?
9. There (goes, go) John and his sister.
10. Ham and eggs (are, is) a tempting dish.
11. Everyone (has, have) some responsibilities.
12. (Doesn't, Don't) either of you girls want this?
13. Each of the pupils (has, have) to make a separate report.
14. (Does, Do) anyone remember the date?
15. Mathematics (is, are) very important if you are going to be an engineer.
16. One of the boys (was, were) an honor student.
17. Movies and parties (is, are) her only interests.
18. There (go, goes) Jane and her mother.
19. There (go, goes) Jack with his brother.
20. Do you believe that riches (make, makes) a man?

Exercise 104: Agreement of Verb with Subject —Part III

Select the verb in parenthesis that agrees in person and number with its subject:

1. There (has, have) been several applicants for the position.
2. When (was, were) you told of the accident?
3. Your answer to the question (doesn't, don't) seem just right.
4. Neither of the men (is, are) responsible for the accident.
5. The trees he planted (was, were) destroyed by the storm.
6. Rod (doesn't, don't) swim well yet.
7. There (was, were) Joe and Grace on the platform.

8. The story about robbers and horse thieves always (amuse, amuses) my little brother.

9. One of the dogs (bring, brings) the mail to me each afternoon.

10. Every child (need, needs) milk to drink.
11. A newspaper and three books (was, were) taken from the desk.
12. (Are, Is) each of the pies the same size?
13. A knowledge of chemistry and physics (was, were) required of all applicants.
14. The girl and her mother always (enter, enters) church early.
15. (Do, Does) any boys want to go fishing tomorrow?
16. Neither of these books (is, are) of any use to me
17. Only one of the boys (is, are) willing to go.
18. Do you want me to tell you if any of your visitors (arrive, arrives)?
19. A box of cigars (was, were) found on the porch.
20. Mathematics (is, are) required of all students.

40. Agreement of Pronoun with Its Antecedent

A pronoun should agree in number, gender and person with its antecedent. The **antecedent** of a pronoun is the word for which the pronoun stands.

> The boy lost *his* sweater.
>   (*his* stands for *boy*)
> Tom and Jack did *their* best.
>   (*their* stands for *Tom* and *Jack*)

The following pronouns are singular and the pronouns that refer to them should be singular in number: every, everybody, everyone, each, nobody, either, neither, one, no one, a person, many a.

> *Everybody* brought *his* lunch.
> *Each* of the girls wants *her* way.

If *one* is used as the antecedent pronoun, the pronoun that refers to it should also be *one's.*

> *One* never gets into trouble when *one* minds *one's* own business.

Exercise 105: Agreement of Pronoun with Its Antecedent—Part I

Select the pronoun in parenthesis that agrees with its antecedent:

1. One of the girls lost (her, their) books.
2. Each of the men did (his, their) duty.
3. Does anyone desire to have (his, their) money refunded?
4. Someone has volunteered (his, their) car for the day.

5. Many a person had to earn (his, their) own living while in college.

6. Every one of us gave (his, our) all to the cause.
7. Neither Helen nor Jane could find (her, their) shoes.
8. Each of the dogs ran to (his, their) master.
9. Nobody wants to do (his, their) work.
10. Nobody had any books with (him, them).
11. Everyone kept (his, their) eyes upon the singer.

12. **Neither** man would give (his, their) name to the officer.
13. **Either** John or James will give me (his, their) version of the accident.
14. **Both** Marie and Joan dressed (her, their) best today.
15. We asked **each** pupil to bring (his, their) own lunch.
16. John, **as well as** the other boys, will do (his, their) job.
17. Sam **and** David tried (his, their) very best.
18. Won't **somebody** please let me have (his, their) pencil for a few minutes?
19. Will **everyone** please open (his, their) book?
20. **Many a** person has said in anger what (he, they) later regretted.

Exercise 106: Agreement of Pronoun with Its Antecedent—Part II

Select the pronoun in parenthesis that agrees with its antecedent:

1. No one may use (his, their) books for this test.
2. Will somebody share (his, their) book with me?
3. Some of the guests brought (his, their) musical instruments.
4. Either you or Louis will lose (his, their) position on the team.

5. If anybody wishes to go, (he, they) may do so now.
6. Everyone must have (his, their) own ticket ready.
7. As they entered the brilliantly lighted church, (he, they) became filled with reverence.
8. The girls prepared (her, their) little introductory speech.
9. Has everyone done (his, their) theme for this week?
10. If anybody has a preference, let (him, them) put his preference in writing.
11. Will each student leave (his, their) assignment on my desk?
12. Neither of them seemed willing to do (his, their) share of the work.
13. Both John and Bob are using (his, their) canoe this morning.
14. Everyone is expected to do (his, their) share on this trip.
15. Every boy was eager to contribute (his, their) bit.
16. If anyone fails, (he, they) must suffer the consequences.
17. Will everyone help (himself, themselves) to the sandwiches?
18. Not one of the dogs hurt (its, their) paws.
19. All guests must leave (his, their) check stub at the door.
20. Each one must prepare (his, their) work carefully.

41. Case of Pronouns

All pronouns are divided into three cases according to their use in a sentence: nominative, objective, possessive.

Person	NOMINATIVE CASE		OBJECTIVE CASE	
	Singular	Plural	Singular	Plural
1st	I	we	me	us
2nd	you	you	you	you
3rd	he, she, it	they	him, her, it	them

Nominative case:

1. Subject of a verb—

   She was right.

   He and *I* are friends. (compound subject)

   Henry is older than *she*. (*is old* is understood)

2. Predicate nominative (after a linking verb)—

   That is *he*.

   It was *she* who called.

193

3. Appositive (after a noun or pronoun in the nominative case)—

   We girls are joining the Y.W.C.A.

   Two boys, Peter and *he,* were called upon.

Objective case:

1. Direct object—

   I saw *him* yesterday.

   Dad took Richard and *me* to the game.

2. Indirect object (after a transitive verb)—

   The teacher read (to) *us* a story.

   I showed (to) *him* the answer.

   He sent (to) my brother and (to) *me* a gift.

3. Object of a preposition—

   May I go with *her?*

   Between you and *me,* I don't like his coat.

   Dad left a dollar for Louise and *me.*

4. Appositive (after a noun or pronoun in the objective case)—

   He spoke to *us* boys.

   The teacher called upon two girls, Joan and *me.*

5. Subject of an infinitive—

   I know *him* to be guilty.

Possessive case:

1. Before a gerund—

   Mother didn't like *my* being out late.

Case of Who and Whom

Who is the nominative form, *whom* the objective.

Use *who* as the subject.

   Who was with you? (subject of *was*)

   Who shall I say wants this? (subject of *wants*)

Use *whom* as the object of a verb and of a preposition.

   Whom does he want? (object of *does want*)

   To *whom* did you address it? (object of *to*)

   I don't know to *whom* he is talking. (object of *to*)

Exercise 107: Case of Pronouns—Part I

Select the correct pronoun in parenthesis:

1. There is no brighter boy than (he, him).

2. I will keep it for you and (he, him).
3. It was (they, them) who arrived late.
4. He reads more fluently than (she, her).
5. They selected (he, him) to represent the team.
6. Who but (her, she) could think of it?
7. May James and (I, me) go with him?
8. If anyone is to remain at home, it will be (I, me).
9. It must have been (we, us) at the door.
10. Everyone but (her, she) plans to go.
11. You are no better than (me, I).
12. That's (he, him).
13. (We, Us) girls had not heard of him.
14. Did you want (her, she) to go with you?

15. Did you resent (his, him) failing to write you?

16. Between you and (I, me), I do not agree.
17. They thought it was (me, I).
18. It was (we, us) who gave the alarm.
19. The man told Ralph and (she, her) to drive on.
20. All except (he, him) are satisfied.

Exercise 108: Case of Pronouns—Part II

Select the correct pronoun in parenthesis:

1. Did he call (us, we) boys?
2. What if Fred and (me, I) don't like it?
3. It looks like (her, she).
4. Mary is as sure as (we, us) that she will win.
5. Who can that be, Jane or (he, him)?
6. I cannot understand (him, his) neglecting to call me yesterday.
7. Has anyone inquired about James and (he, him)?
8. If I were (she, her), I would be ashamed.
9. Who else wants some? (Us, We).
10. Don't ask (him, he) to do it.
11. Whom did they help, you or (he, him)?
12. They met Peter and (I, me) at the door.
13. You and (I, me) shall go to the movies.
14. All but (he, him) were invited.
15. Did you expect (she, her) to come today?
16. It was (I, me) whom you saw, but it was (she, her) who left the room.
17. Did Mother approve of (your, you) going to the game Saturday?
18. For John and (she, her), all subjects seem easy.
19. Who could have said that about Kate and (I, me)?
20. Who did that, you or (her, she)?

Exercise 109: Case of Pronouns—Part III

Select the correct pronoun in parenthesis:

1. The mailman had letters for (he, him) and (I, me).
2. The club invited Mr. Sparks and (I, me) to the banquet.
3. I do not know the road as well as (she, her).
4. (We, Us) boys don't like the work.
5. He is not as old as (she, her).
6. I asked (her, she) to be my partner.
7. Give it to (us, we) boys.
8. I did not hear of (you, your) winning the prize.
9. Have you seen him and (her, she)?
10. It was (he, him) who called the police.
11. I am not as good a player as (she, her).
12. If you were (her, she), would you accept?
13. Please tell (they, them) to wait for me in my room.
14. He told it to Lucy and (I, me).
15. Bill and (I, me) are good friends.
16. Everyone except (they, them) was there.
17. I am afraid that Martha and (she, her) are lost.
18. You may give the money to either Mother or (me, I).
19. I am grateful for (your, you) driving me home in this rain.
20. Who was there, you or (she, her)?

Exercise 110: Case of Pronouns—Part IV

Select the correct pronoun in parenthesis:

1. She told the story to Edna and (they, them).
2. Uncle Albert sent my sister and (me, I) a present.
3. Two boys, Tom and (him, he), were absent today.
4. The girl is shorter than (he, him).
5. Laura and (she, her) are classmates.
6. I offered (he, him) one of my sandwiches.
7. When shall (we, us) girls eat lunch?
8. Had you heard of (me, my) getting a new position?
9. I asked (he, him) to go to the store for me.
10. You may go with either Joseph or (I, me).
11. All the girls except (she, her) went to the dance.
12. Is Janice younger than (her, she)?
13. The principal gave medals to two boys, Sam and (he, him).
14. Dad does not approve of (you, your) working so late.
15. Who called me, you or (he, him)?
16. Do you believe it was (them, they) who wrote?
17. The two friends, Gladys and (her, she), went for a walk.
18. Martin and (me, I) went swimming together.
19. (Us, We) friends should remain loyal to each other.
20. Who received the note, (her, she) or (him, he)?

Exercise 111: Case of Who and Whom—Part I

Insert *who* or *whom* in each of the following blanks:

1. _____ do you want, Mary?
2. You are the one _____ is at fault.
3. Do you know _____ is going to help?
4. Here is a boy _____ we all know very well.
5. To _____ are you speaking?
6. I do not know _____ rang the bell.
7. He asked me _____ rang.
8. For _____ did you call?
9. _____ shall it be?
10. To _____ are you referring?
11. Was he the one _____ failed?
12. I don't know _____ gave him the job.
13. _____ did he appoint?
14. I do not see anyone _____ was present.
15. The boy _____ was at the desk left this.
16. Jerry is one _____ always studies.
17. With _____ was he talking?
18. _____ could it have been?
19. Here is a man _____ knows his business.
20. Here is a person _____ everybody likes.

Exercise 112: Case of Who and Whom—Part I

Insert *who* or *whom* in each of the following blanks:

1. Can you guess _____ it is?
2. I don't know to _____ they are talking.
3. To _____ did the note refer?
4. _____ do you think it is?
5. _____ did he say it is?
6. Can it be he _____ they mean?
7. There are men _____ are classified as skilled workers.
8. _____ shall I call for tomorrow?
9. _____ did you refer to as the brightest in the class?
10. _____ did they appoint secretary of the club?
11. _____ are you thinking of, Mary?
12. For _____ are you knitting that?
13. _____ do you think did this?
14. _____ is there?
15. _____ do you think it was _____ left these papers here?
16. _____ did he mean?
17. To _____ does this book belong?
18. I saw the girl to _____ you gave the sweater.
19. Guess _____ it was.
20. _____ was it _____ showed us about the grounds?

Exercise 113: Review of Case—Part I

Select the correct pronoun in parenthesis:

1. There was no one at home except (they, them).
2. It was (they, them) who broke the window.
3. (Who, Whom) shall we blame?
4. It must have been (they, them) in the car.
5. It wasn't (us, we) anyway.
6. We expected (him, he) to be scolded.
7. From (who, whom) did you get that shirt?
8. In front of the boathouse sat Sam and (he, him).
9. Only two of (us, we) boys were invited.
10. Some of (us, we) pupils don't like her.
11. Was it (he, him) whom I met?
12. Francis is shorter than (he, him).
13. (Us, We) two boys are very close friends.
14. Can't you ask Jane and (he, him) to do the work?
15. I don't see anyone (whom, who) knows me.
16. I appreciate (you, your) taking me home.
17. It must have been (he, him) with the boys.
18. What do you want (us, we) boys and girls to do about it?
19. (Who, Whom) are you writing to, Alice?
20. Everyone but John and (he, him) was ready when we arrived.

Exercise 114: Review of Case—Part II

Select the correct pronoun in parenthesis:

1. If I were (she, her), I wouldn't say a word about it.
2. Yes, it is at (her, she) that I was aiming my remarks.
3. I don't know just what I would do if I were (he, him).
4. What do you think of (him, his) leaving so early?
5. (Him, He) and I will go when the time comes.
6. To (we, us) pupils it was wonderful news.
7. Won't you come with (we, us) boys?
8. I wonder (who, whom) ate the cake.
9. Mary plays much better than (I, me).
10. All were excluded except (us, we) three.
11. (Whom, Who) shall we invite?
12. I don't like (their, them) leaving him alone all day.
13. Among (us, we) four girls, there will always be a deep friendship.
14. Divide it between Gene and (he, him).
15. The ones on the phone were (we, us) boys.
16. It must have been (he, him) whom they meant
17. For (who, whom) did you bring this gift?
18. Father criticized (me, my) doing my homework while playing the radio.
19. (Who, Whom) do you think I met yesterday?
20. (He, Him) and Jerry are always together.

42. *Impersonal Pronouns (It, You, They)*

In most sentences, the pronouns *it, you* and *they* need antecedents. However, when the pronoun *it* is not intended to refer to any antecedent, it is said to be used impersonally, as in the following sentences:

> *It* was a warm day.
>
> I hope *it* will be cooler.
>
> They roughed *it* for a week.
>
> Because of the wind, we were hard put to *it*.

In the following sentences, *it* needs an antecedent.

> *Wrong:* In a recent book, it says that this town was built over a hundred years ago.
>
> *Right:* In a recent book, the author states that this town was built over a hundred years ago.

The pronoun *you* is sometimes used indefinitely, not referring to any particular person.

> In reading fiction, *you* identify yourself with the hero and heroine. (*you* = one)

The pronoun *they* is sometimes used indefinitely, meaning "people in general."

> *They* said Columbus was a dreamer who imagined the earth was round. (*They* = people in general)
> *Wrong:* They produce much rubber in Brazil.
> *Right:* The people of Brazil produce much rubber.

Exercise 115: Impersonal Pronouns

Correct each of the following sentences:

1. They refine sugar at Fellsmere.
2. In our school paper, it showed John just as he fell into the water.

3. In "Ivanhoe" it tells about tournaments.

4. In Florida and California they raise oranges, tangerines and grapefruit.
5. In "The Ransom of Red Chief" it tells about a boy who was kidnaped.

43. *The Articles*

There are two articles: *the* and *a* (or *an*).

The dance was held last week.

A dance was held last week.

In the first sentence, it is quite clear that a certain particular dance is referred to. It is a definite dance which is spoken of. Therefore, *the* is called the **definite article.**

In the second sentence, no particular dance is referred to. The reference as to what dance is referred to is indefinite. Therefore, *a* is called the **indefinite article.** The article *a* also has the form *an*.

A is used before words beginning with a consonant sound. *An* is used before words beginning with a vowel or vowel sound.

> an aviator, an express office, an hour, a history, a package, a European country (notice that European begins with a consonant sound)

The word *hour* begins with a vowel sound. The *h* in *hour* is silent, so we say *an hour*. In *history* the *h* is not silent but nearly so, so we say *an historical* lecture.

> an heir, an honest boy, a hotel, a holiday

Since the indefinite article, *a, an,* has the numerical meaning of *one,* it should never be used after expressions such as *sort of* and *kind of.*

> Do you like this sort of movie?
> *not:*
> Do you like this sort of a (or one) movie?

> What kind of rug is that?
> *not:*
> What kind of a (or one) rug is that?

Exercise 116: The Articles

Select the correct *article* in parenthesis:

1. He took (a, an) package to the office.
2. (A, An) aviator flew the plane.
3. We stopped at (a, an) hotel.
4. He surely is (a, an) hustler.
5. Last week we had (a, an) hot wave.
6. We will have (a, an) holiday on April 26.
7. We will use (a, an) herb* to make the medicine.
8. We did not receive (a, an) ounce of sugar.
9. They will remain in (a, an) European port.
10. He was named as (a, an) heir to the estate.

---

* *herb* is pronounced ûrb and also hûrb. Webster give⁻ ûrb as preferred.

44. *Comparison of Adjectives and Adverbs*

Comparison of Adjectives

Adjectives have three degrees of comparison: positive, comparative, superlative.

The **positive degree** is used in describing *one* person or object.

He is a *tall* boy.

The **comparative degree** is used in comparing *two* persons or objects, or in comparing the same person or object at two different times.

He is the *taller* of the two boys.

Mary is *prettier* now than she was last summer.

The **superlative degree** is used in comparing *three or more* persons or objects, or to mean *extremely* or *very*.

He is the *tallest* boy in the class.

She is a *most agreeable* girl.

Most one-syllable adjectives and many two-syllable adjectives form the comparative by adding *er,* and the superlative by adding *est.*

short, shorter, shortest   clever, cleverer, cleverest

With adjectives of three syllables or more, and those that would be hard to pronounce with *er* and *est* endings, use *more* to form the comparative and *most* to form the superlative.

Positive: dangerous
Comparative: *more* dangerous
Superlative: *most* dangerous

Some adjectives are compared irregularly.

Positive	Comparative	Superlative
good, well	better	best
much, many	more	most
~ld	older, elder	oldest, eldest
bad, ill	worse	worst
far	farther, further	farthest, furthest

COMPARISON OF ADVERBS

Regular adverbs follow the same rules as those given for regular adjectives in forming the three degrees of comparison.

Usually if the adverb does not end in *ly*, the comparative degree is formed by adding *er*, and the superlative by adding *est*.

>   *Positive:*   late
>   *Comparative:* later
>   *Superlative:* latest

Most adverbs ending in *ly* form the comparative degree by the use of *more,* and the superlative by *most.*

>   *Positive:*   loudly
>   *Comparative:* *more* loudly
>   *Superlative:* *most* loudly

A few adverbs are compared irregularly.

Positive	*Comparative*	*Superlative*
little	less	least
badly, ill	worse	worst
well	better	best
much	more	most

Because of their meaning, some adjectives and adverbs cannot be compared: absolutely, daily, endless, entirely, eternally, faultless, first, immaculate, immediately, level, previously, priceless, singly, somewhat, square, supreme, unique, unanimous.

ERRORS TO AVOID

Don't use both methods of comparison together.

The sky is *bluer* today.

(Don't use *more bluer*.)

Use the *comparative* degree when comparing *two* persons or things, the *superlative* when comparing *more than two* persons or things.

Paul is the *taller* of the *two* boys.

Louise is the *tallest* of the *three* girls.

When comparing members of a group, use *else* or *other* with the comparative, *all* with the superlative.

Ann is *taller* than anyone *else* in her class.

or: Ann is *taller* than any *other* girl in her class.

or: Ann is the *tallest* of *all* the girls in her class.

or: Ann is the *tallest* girl in her class.

Exercise 117: Comparison of Adjectives and Adverbs—Part I

Compare the following adjectives and adverbs:

1. icy	8. loud	15. frightened
2. bright	9. well	16. necessary
3. quiet	10. ill	17. little
4. soon	11. young	18. ugly
5. candid	12. low	19. much
6. silent	13. magnificent	20. bad
7. careful	14. cheap	

Exercise 118: Comparison of Adjectives and Adverbs—Part II

Compare the following adjectives and adverbs:

1. slow	8. much	15. far
2. steadily	9. wasteful	16. great
3. well	10. happy	17. wicked
4. beautiful	11. bad	18. little
5. generously	12. merry	19. noisy
6. brilliant	13. surprising	20. charitable
7. fresh	14. green	

Exercise 119: Comparison of Adjectives and Adverbs—Part III

Some of the following sentences are correct, others incorrect. Rewrite those which are incorrect.

1. This is the most sweetest candy of all.
2. She is the more older of the two.
3. This is the worstest suit in the store.
4. Helen is the younger of the three girls.

5. The city is three miles farther.

6. This is the greenest grass I have ever seen.
7. Myrna is the smartest of the twins.
8. The ambitionest girl in the class is Louise.
9. Joan is the beautifuller of the two.
10. Martin is shorter than any boy in his class.
11. She is the most contented person I have ever known
12. Louise is much taller now than a year ago.
13. Our school has the bestest football team in the state
14. This is the sharper of all the knives.
15. Phil is the more better hitter on the team.
16. All the money was left to the eldest son.
17. Mother feels weller than yesterday.
18. Since that day we quarreled, I like her lesser.
19. She is a most friendly girl.
20. He is a better runner than any man on the team.

45. Double Negatives

Do not use in the same sentence two or more negative words. Two negatives contradict each other and make an affirmative. *I haven't got no paper* means that you do have some paper.

Say: I don't want *any* (not *no*) cereal.

There aren't *any* (not *no*) apples in the dish.

Do not use in the same sentence any of the following words with another negative word: no, never, scarcely, hardly, only, but (meaning only), none, nobody, no one, nothing, neither, not (or n't).

Say: He didn't have *any* (not *none*).

John hasn't *any* (not *no*) book.

They *have* (not *haven't*) none.

We *were* (not *weren't*) *hardly* able to sleep.

Exercise 120: Double Negatives—Part I

Copy the following sentences, making all necessary corrections. A few are correct as they stand.

1. He doesn't have no paper.
2. I haven't nothing to sell.
3. They haven't nobody to play with.
4. I hadn't never seen him before.
5. I didn't see him nowhere.
6. John didn't eat neither vegetable.
7. Are you sure you haven't lost anything?

8. I've never seen no rodeo.

9. I don't have no books to read.
10. Neil hadn't never heard of the book.
11. Mother couldn't hardly hear me.
12. I haven't no time for such things.
13. I have never seen any submarines.
14. There wasn't no opportunity to study.
15. I am sure I haven't dropped nothing on the way.
16. He isn't hardly able to swim to shore.
17. I didn't find nobody at home.
18. I haven't any appetite, Mother.
19. I am sure he won't go nowhere.
20. She didn't like none of these.

Exercise 121: Double Negatives—Part II

Copy the following sentences, making all necessary corrections. A few are correct as they stand.

1. I couldn't hardly speak.
2. She hasn't no money.
3. Ralph didn't have but one chance at the prize.
4. I am sure they didn't have no other plans.
5. Mother can hardly hear me from my room.
6. Rex won't bite nobody.
7. I am sure she hasn't no books for us.
8. I didn't seen no one I know at the game.
9. She hasn't done nothing today.
10. He didn't have no money.
11. They don't need any now.
12. William didn't see nobody around.
13. Can't you find no butter?
14. He was not permitted to go nowhere.
15. Mother says she can't never depend on him.
16. The boys haven't any relatives in this country.
17. It wasn't hardly noon when we set out.
18. After all, they weren't hardly surprised.
19. There wasn't nobody in school so late.
20. It was so warm the dog couldn't scarcely move

46. *Singular and Plural Number*

The **singular number** of a noun is the form that signifies only *one* person, place or thing.

The **plural number** of a noun is the form that signifies *more than one* person, place or thing.

Rules for Forming the Plural of Nouns

1. Most nouns form their plural by adding *s* to the singular.

   girl—girls   hat—hats

   friend—friends   spoonful—spoonfuls

2. Some nouns ending with the sounds *s, sh, ch* or **x** form their plural by adding *es* to the singular.

   guess—guesses   radish—radishes

   watch—watches   ax—axes

3. Nouns ending in *y*, preceded by a vowel, form their plural by adding *s* to the singular.

   day—days   toy—toys

4. Nouns ending in *y*, preceded by a consonant, form their plural by changing *y* to *i* and adding *es*.

    army—armies   baby—babies

5. Most nouns ending in *o* add only *s* to form the plural.

    solo—solos   radio—radios

    piano—pianos   portfolio—portfolios

6. Some nouns ending in *o* add *es* to form the plural.

    hero—heroes   veto—vetoes

    Negro—Negroes potato—potatoes

7. Most nouns ending with the sound of *f* add *s* to form the plural.

    cliff—cliffs   roof—roofs

    chief—chiefs   proof—proofs

8. Some nouns ending with the sound of *f* change the *f* or *fe* to *v* and add *es* to form the plural

    wife—wives   life—lives

    loaf—loaves   calf—calves

9. Some nouns are used only in the plural.

    measles, mumps, trousers, shears scissors, riches, oats, goods

10. The nouns *athletics, news, mathematics, physics* and *politics* are always plural in form although singular in meaning. (*Example:* There *is* good *news* tonight.)

11. Some nouns form their plural by a change in spelling.

woman—women   mouse—mice

ox—oxen   foot—feet

child—children   goose—geese

12. Some nouns have the same form in both the singular and plural.

deer, sheep, trout, swine, salmon, Chinese, corps

13. Usually compound nouns form their plural by making the principal word plural, but sometimes both parts are made plural.

editor-in-chief—editors-in-chief

mother-in-law—mothers-in-law

man-of-war—men-of-war

man servant—men servants

Exercise 122: Singular and Plural Number– Part I

Write the *plural* of the following nouns:

1. wish	11. family	21. ax
2. city	12. house	22. athletics
3. fisherman	13. roof	23. proof
4. victory	14. half	24. tooth
5. life	15. party	25. commander-in-chief
6. tomato	16. box	26. patch
7. sister-in-law	17. cliff	27. story
8. place	18. fireman	28. penny
9. army	19. goose	29. spoonful
10. deer	20. chief	30. foot

Exercise 123: Singular and Plural Number– Part II

Write the *plural* of the following nouns:

1. tax	11. knife	21. cupful
2. salesman	12. valley	22. son-in-law
3. wife	13. piano	23. motorman
4. leaf	14. Frenchman	24. child
5. hero	15. baby	25. lily
6. tooth	16. lady-in-waiting	26. news
7. self	17. sheep	27. woman
8. Negro	18. cry	28. mouse
9. foot	19. puff	29. ox
10. echo	20. potato	30. loss

Exercise 124: Singular and Plural Number--Part III

Write the *plural* of the following nouns:

1. calf	11. policeman	21. politics
2. princess	12. life	22. veto
3. paper	13. glass	23. portfolio
4. tax	14. buffalo	24. cliff
5. roof	15. piano	25. box
6. joy	16. baby	26. play
7. hero	17. teaspoonful	27. sheep
8. radio	18. chief	28. editor-in-chief
9. army	19. switch	29. tomato
10. potato	20. Chinese	30. plateful

47. *The Apostrophe to Show Possession and Contraction*

To use the apostrophe to show possession, (*a*) select the word which shows ownership, (*b*) add an apostrophe to this word, and (*c*) add an *s* if the word does not already end in *s*.

In *The girl's hat was lost,* the word which shows ownership is *girl* because one girl is implied. Add the apostrophe to the word: *girl'*. Here the word does not end in *s*, so an *s* is added: *girl's*.

In *Ladies' hats were on sale,* the word which does the possessing is *ladies* because more than one lady is implied. Add an apostrophe to the word: *ladies'*. Here the word ends in *s*, so *s* is not added.

If you have difficulty in finding the word which does the possessing, change the possessive into an *of*-phrase. In the first sentence above, it would be *the hat of the girl.* In the second sentence, it would be *the hats of the ladies.*

To show joint possession, add the apostrophe to the last name only in a pair or a series.

Boyle and Farr's.   Tom, Fred and Joe's side won

To show separate ownership, add the apostrophe to each name.

Brown's and Jason's.

Nouns which name inanimate things form their possessive by using an *of*-phrase.

the cover of the book (*not* the book's cover)

There are a few exceptions to the last-mentioned **rule:**

1. Expressions of *measure:*

a dollar's worth   fifty cents' worth

2. Expressions of *time:*

yesterday's news   two days' vacation

3. Expressions of *personification:*

(In personification an idea or a thing is spoken of as if it were a person.)

the world's advancement

Caution: Possessive pronouns never take the apostrophe since they are already in the possessive case.

whose, its, yours, ours, theirs, hers

The apostrophe is used in contractions to show where letters are omitted.

don't (do not)   it's (it is)

doesn't (does not)   he's (he is)

I'll (I will)   aren't (are not)

Exercise 125: The Apostrophe to Show Possession and Contraction—Part I

Rewrite correctly those words which require an *apostrophe:*

1. He received a months vacation.
2. A freshmans cap was found on the ground.
3. I will help in my fathers business.
4. The ladys coat was torn.

5. Napoleon's achievements were many.

6. He did a mans work.
7. Dont you know the answer to Lewis question?
8. Mens and boys hats were everywhere.
9. Have you seen a boys coat anywhere?
10. It was my mothers good luck to find a watch.
11. Ill see you at Bills house tonight.

12. Two small boys toys lay all about.
13. Her two sisters children
14. Two weeks pay
15. A sailors life is very interesting.
16. Todays paper is here.
17. The worlds progress
18. My two parents influence
19. Her only sisters children
20. Two girls books

Exercise 126: The Apostrophe to Show Possession and Contraction—Part II

Rewrite correctly those words which require an *apostrophe:*

1. My cousins watch was lost.
2. The directors office has been redecorated.
3. Marys health is much improved.
4. I read some of Scotts poems.
5. Is this Lewis book?
6. The new ship is the Navys pride.
7. Is this yours, or is it Helens?
8. Charles home is in Ocala, while Joes is in Rochester.
9. Werent you tired last night?
10. Wouldnt you like Phils books?
11. Whats the matter?
12. Its too bad that the dog hurt its foot, isnt it?

13. Give me a nickels worth of candy and two cents worth of gum.

14. Four years college training fits you for your lifes work.

15. The boys carried the girls packages for them.

16. Did you get three weeks pay for a months work?

17. All the other girls got their mothers consent easily, but my mothers approval came hard.

18. This is ours, not Johns.

19. The days work was soon begun.

20. He hung up a deers head.

Exercise 127: The Apostrophe to Show Possession and Contraction—Part III

Rewrite correctly those words which require an *apostrophe:*

1. A dimes worth of candy

2. Five cents worth of gum

3. This is all he has to show for a years work.

4. For pitys sake, dont do that.

5. Barker and Wheelers Store (joint ownership)
6. Barkers Store and Wheelers Store (separate ownership)
7. Doesnt he know its wrong?
8. These are ours, arent they?
9. The teachers classbook was not in its place.
10. Did the boys hat lie beside yours?
11. Who will take Joes place?
12. Here is a mans coat and seven pairs of womens gloves.
13. Do you enjoy speaking before womens clubs?
14. Nobody elses trouble seemed so disturbing as hers.
15. Are these Freds or theirs?
16. Which do you like better, Keats long poems or Burns short ones?
17. The two boys dinner was on the table

18. Shouldnt we help to bear one anothers burdens?

19. The childs hat is lost, isnt it?
20. The childrens old toys were packed together with the new ones.

48. The Use of Who, Which, What, That

Who and *whom* refer to persons.

> *Who* took the book? *Whom* do you wish to see?

Which and *what* refer to animals and things.

> *Which* dog is yours?   *What* a day!

That refers to persons, animals and things.

> The man *that* called you is my brother.

> The school *that* I attend has a library.

Note that *what* never has an antecedent.

> This is the hat *which* (not *what*) I had lost.

Exercise 128: The Use of Who, Which, What, That

Select the word in parenthesis that correctly completes each sentence.

1. My brother has many friends in college, one of (which, whom) goes to Yale.

2. Last year I saw a game (which, what) I have not yet forgotten.
3. Lucky is he (who, which) has many friends.
4. The two boys (what, who) were camping on the Gulf are now home.
5. One of the women (that, which) works for us is on her vacation.
6. This dog is the most intelligent animal (what, that) I have ever known.
7. Where is the radio (what, which) Uncle Martin bought you?
8. Is this the cat (that, what) you like?
9. There are fifteen boys on the squad, six of (which, whom) are substitutes.
10. The boys (which, that) I met are in my class.

49. Gender

Gender is the form of the noun or pronoun that denotes sex.

Masculine gender denotes the male sex. Many masculine nouns end in *er* and *or*.

boy, he, rooster, master, emperor

Feminine gender denotes the female sex. Many feminine nouns end in *ess*.

girl, she, hen, mistress, empress

Common gender denotes either the male or female sex.

teacher, pupil, cat, dog, I, you

Neuter gender is used for inanimate (non-living) objects and for the lower forms of animate (living) life.

desk, it, lizard, snake, star

Exercise 129: Gender

Select the nouns and pronouns and state whether each is *masculine* (use M), *feminine* (F), *common* (C) or *neuter* (N) *gender:*

1. The king sent the queen some gifts.
2. The leader said that we must attend.
3. The boys coasted their bikes down the long hill.
4. Who found it?
5. John, you will find the newspaper on the table in the living room.
6. Has anyone seen Mary or Henry?
7. At the assembly today, our principal spoke on the topic of safety.
8. The child lost her toys.
9. Who is your best friend?
10. The writer of the book is a woman.
11. Sally and Ted built a boat.
12. Have you ever given sugar to a horse?
13. Did they go with Father and Mother to the movies?
14. He is my pal.
15. We saw Mr. Frank, my teacher, walking down tne street with his dog, Princess.
16. We found a black snake on the lawn.
17. The hen in our yard was given to me by my aunt.
18. The waiter brought us our sandwiches and milk.
19. The girls went with Miss Adams, the boys with Mr. Otis.
20. Robert, who is the boy who called you?

50. *Numerals*

Dates, page numbers and street numbers should be written in figures.

>We came here on November 16, 1944.

>Please turn to page 85.

>They live at 242 Lakeview Avenue.

Spell out a number in a sentence if it may be done in one or two words.

>I earned a hundred dollars.

A long mixed number should be written in figures if it requires the spelling of several words.

>We sold 4357 copies of our school paper.

Never begin a sentence with figures

>Thirteen is an unlucky number.

The dollar sign ($) is used for an amount more than one dollar; spell out an amount for less than one dollar

>You may buy it for forty cents.

>The tickets cost $2.50 each.

Numbers representing the hour of the day or the age
f a person are usually written out.

The train arrives at eleven o'clock.

He is nineteen years old.

Exercise 130: Numerals

Answer the following questions by writing complete
sentences:

1. How old are you?

2. What is your date of birth?
3. What is your address?
4. At what time do you usually arise?
5. How much money do you have with you?

Mastery Test — I

Some of the following sentences are correct and others contain errors in grammar, sentence structure, spelling, capitalization or punctuation. Rewrite only those that are incorrect.

1. The ball must have broke the window.
2. He is a better player than you or me.
3. The boys played ball the girls swam in the pool.
4. There isn't but one good road home from here.
5. Ladies dresses and boys coats were on sale.
6. Sarah doesn't know who she was talking to on the telephone.
7. Neither my father nor my mother are at home.
8. Here is a young bird who cannot fly yet.
9. Yeast makes bread raise.
10. Hoping this finds you well.
11. He divided the work between Joe and me.
12. The uss missouri a battleship is anchored in the harbor.
13. We planted potatos, string beans and tomatos in our garden.
14. Let's not go anywhere because Mother may want us to help her do the housework.

15. I will either go east this summer or spend a month at our camp north of atlanta.
16. This is the most sourest grapefruit I have ever eaten.
17. Everybody was allowed to read their own essay.
18. We used to watch the sun as it set from our porch.
19. Did you expect it to be he?
20. Laying aside his pipe, he took a nap.

Mastery Test — II

Some of the following sentences are correct and others contain errors in grammar, sentence structure, spelling, capitalization or punctuation. Rewrite only those that are incorrect.

1. Please bring this letter to the office.
2. The manager wants Beatrice and I to usher tonight.
3. Haven't you never been in a plane before?
4. Looking out of our kitchen window, the horses were grazing in the meadow.
5. My mother, as well as the children, did their part in cleaning the house.
6. Finally, he lay down to rest for a while; he was very tired.
7. Who is calling she asked.
8. Many visitors come here each year, some have been coming for years.
9. The agent had shown us many samples.

10. Measles are a common disease among children.
11. This is the list apples oranges bananas and lemons.
12. Who is at the door? It is me.
13. Can you guess whom I was talking to this morning?
14. She is more taller than he.
15. Unless someone goes with me.
16. These are interesting books about the lifes of famous heros.
17. Mother finally consented to let me go camping and taking us there in the car.
18. Doesn't he know it's wrong?
19. He studies spanish, art, english and music.
20. I wonder who he will select as chairman.

Mastery Test — III

Some of the following sentences are correct and others contain errors in grammar, sentence structure, spelling, capitalization or punctuation. Rewrite only those that are incorrect.

1. The night was beautiful we walked to the pier.
2. Whom can it be?
3. Neither the principal nor the superintendent has left their forwarding address.
4. Didnt you know Bess father arrived yesterday?
5. There I said is just the dress Im looking for.
6. The money was left for you and me.

7. I don't suppose he has went home yet.
8. Sunday morning I laid in bed until it was time **for** church.
9. I saw two boys, one of which seemed to be badly hurt.
10. Walking along the road, a fire was discovered
11. No one has stole them, I am sure.
12. I don't hardly see how it works that way.
13. My brother is the bestest player on the team.
14. The junior red cross invited miss adams to speak.
15. Mother has consented to them going to camp for the summer.
16. Do you want this kind of a hat?
17. "When, do you suppose, will Mary come home?" Dad asked.
18. One boy with red hair and one with blond hair.
19. The echos were heard in the vallies below.
20. Each of you have worked well.

Mastery Test — IV

Some of the following sentences are correct and others contain errors in grammar, sentence structure, spelling, capitalization or punctuation. Rewrite only those that are incorrect.

1. If Mother had been at home, we would have ate earlier.

2. I don't know whom is to act in my place.
3. Going down the street, a large oak spread its shady branches.
4. A pair of skates were his most welcome gift.
5. You wouldn't expect to find anyone playing tennis on this kind of day.
6. I like to play bridge and reading books.
7. Many books were found lying on the floor.
8. When valuable information was received.
9. After we had set the table, we set down to rest.
10. What do you think of me traveling with Ted to Aunt Ellen's house?
11. Marys mother exclaimed, "Thats ours!"
12. Must you leave so early asked Dad.
13. If anyone finds my keys, will they please return them to me.
14. Did you attend the rally given by the democratic club?
15. This could easily be done by you and me.
16. Betty is the younger of the three girls.
17. The two attorney-at-laws had studied at different universitys.
18. We arrived there at last we could find no place to set up our tent.
19. The man wouldn't scarcely listen to me.
20. What did you expect we boys to do about it?

Mastery Test — V

Some of the following sentences are correct and others contain errors in grammar, sentence structure, spelling, capitalization or punctuation. Rewrite only those that are incorrect.

1. She plays the piano better than me.
2. If the story is a mystery Frances said Ill like it.
3. Near the wharfs lived the familys of the fishermans.
4. One or two boys are needed in the auditorium.
5. Although not everyone likes mashed potatoes.
6. What kind of a car did your brother buy?
7. Let's ride two miles farther.
8. He always praises those which do good work.
9. Ladies shoes are usually more expensive than mens.
10. We expect to attend st james church on christmas eve.
11. I was about to ask you and she to come with me.
12. Whom is it that you most admire?
13. A box of cigars were given Dad on his birthday.
14. The firemen had risen the ladder to the window.
15. I am sure they haven't anything for us.
16. For him and I, Dad left two dollars on the desk.
17. What's the matter can't you find your homework?
18. Does these farmers sell their products in the city?
19. Has the bell rang yet?
20. Walking down the lane, a huge dog confronted us.

Mastery Test — VI

Some of the following sentences are correct and others contain errors in grammar, sentence structure, spelling, capitalization or punctuation. Rewrite only those that are incorrect.

1. I worked at a camp last year to earn some money and so that I could be near the water.
2. They drove to hollywood which is north of us.
3. A box of apples was sent us by Uncle William.
4. Who ever dreamed of him winning both prizes?
5. Laura is the smartest of the twin sisters.
6. Because I had never been there before.
7. Mother, may I lie down for a while.
8. He who you saw on the stage is my friend.
9. Each of the players knew their place.
10. In front of the house, youll see a sign, "Keep off other peoples property."
11. While eating my dinner, a dog came to the door.
12. The secretary and treasurer is Joe Williams.
13. It seems that we can't go nowhere tonight.
14. In the storys, the two firemans became heros.
15. "I am tired of your playing the radio so much," she said.
16. We had drove fifty miles before lunch.
17. No one could read as quickly as she.
18. May I bring this to the library?

19. Never they said will we give up.
20. I ran to pick up the child, fortunately he was not injured.

Mastery Test — VII

Some of the following sentences are correct and others contain errors in grammar, sentence structure, spelling, capitalization or punctuation. Rewrite only those that are incorrect.

1. Lie the groceries on the floor.
2. Between you and she, there is no comparison.
3. I ran to the corner, then I turned in the alarm.
4. Many a person has said that which they did not mean.
5. Its packed with sheeps wool.
6. Have any of the letters been answered yet?
7. Well that settles it said mother.
8. The two young childs were given candys by their mothers.
9. My shirt has shrank.
10. Who will you send with the packages, and whom will be there to receive them?
11. He put the candy in a dish which he later ate.
12. She hasn't only a few minutes in which to finish it.
13. The teacher asked everyone to keep his eyes on his own work.

14. I sat the package on the floor and set down to rest for a while.
15. Barry is the tallest and heaviest boy in the class.
16. Yes, we dont have any school on washingtons birthday nor on lincolns.
17. I expected Henry to be lonesome and that he would want to go home.
18. I dropped the plate; it broke into hundreds of little pieces.
19. Did you look forward to she coming home?
20. After he had eaten two oranges.

Index